With Reference

SCDA—Notions of Space

Soo K. Chan

ORO EDITIONS

With Reference

I
Notions of Space

"Space" is an immeasurable and unfixed term. Its meaning is impossible to define in a singular manner, yet everyone has a perception of its value. Space is a physical parameter; it captures a volumetric reading. It is, however, also a conceptual notion. In this way, we can see architecture in particular, as both enclosing space and giving an *idea* of space.

Space was not used as an architectural term before the late 1800s. Previously a word common only within philosophical discourse, in architecture, the term was introduced as part of the development of modernism and its terminology still dominates our lexicon.[1]

In fact, notions of space are the basis of nearly all theories that have shaped the past century of architectural movements—whether as reactions against or extensions of the spatial propositions of modernism. Space will continue to be a shifting concept that, precisely in its undefined nature, offers much opportunity for exploration and experimentation.

In the following pages, we're as much interested in space as in the relationships between spaces. To encapsulate as broad an understanding of space as possible, we rely both on more classically rooted terminology that evokes ideas of space—such as procession, order, enclosure, transitions—and more contemporary terms like "spatial plasticity," a consideration of the relationship of spaces to each other and to the whole.

The space for living is the most fundamental, and by extension how we live together—within units, within buildings, within cities, and within the world—must be very carefully considered. Many notable architects in modern history have reimagined the future of residential space. Le Corbusier saw the house as a machine for living, while Mies van der Rohe brought in light through precision and assemblage, developing the curtainwall, and Frank Lloyd Wright strove for an integration of organic architecture and nature. We can learn from each of these precedents—some strategies work and some do not.

Over the years, SCDA has had similar opportunity to rethink high density housing, with projects in different locations with different climates, and with different budgets to test these ideas. It has urged us to examine what the most pressing concerns are, regardless of the site-specific parameters of each project.

With projects all over the world, we know that one singular strategy will never make for a successful solution. However, our basic needs are universal. We can rely on the fact that the quality of our spatial environments impacts our health: light and air are required for our wellbeing; and we cannot live in artificial silos, we need to be connected to nature in some way.

In the following pages, we have gathered 10 projects, spanning over 20 years, to explore how we design and put buildings together. Assessing one's own work is often a worthy and illuminating exercise. In past publications, we have felt the luxury of receiving outside perspectives. Aaron Betsky has characterized SCDA's practice as one suspended between emerging technology and different cultures,[2] while Leon van Schaik has argued for a distancing from these dual realities. He instead suggests a utopian search for perfection—in each work, seeking the realization of a *gesamtkunstwerk*;[3] no matter the context, practice makes perfect. It is not implausible that the two characterizations could be seen working in unison. While Betsky regards SCDA as a "ruthless and effective scavenger of whatever organizational principles"[4] are deemed appropriate for the situation at hand, van Schaik observes how "messy reality is edited out" in our work; he states that our "idealism drives an architectural toolkit," comprising "orthogonal relationships between literal and phenomenal transparency of horizontal and vertical planes, the floating of rectangular volumes and tabula rasa recasting of the ground and water planes, and the creation of over-sailing sky planes."[5]

Both authors may be right in some way, I suspect. Certainly, SCDA was born as an amalgamation of movements and multiple localities, but it is also a consistent response to the plurality of demands and externalities that pervade commissioned work today.

Having designed single-family residences and high-rise towers, cultural institutions and commercial properties, a persistent interest in spatiality becomes clear in the range of work. In fact, as is evident in the following pages, clear traces of the spatial principles we experimented with in early residences can be found in our multi-unit housing structures.

In examining our projects—completed, on the boards, and those that remained as sketches and ideas—I would propose that our work is intentionally not about singular definitions. Perhaps this approach is rooted in my education as an architect during an academically "permissive" environment in the 1980s, a moment defined by pluralistic tendencies, when we all found excitement and opportunism in a promiscuity of thought. I have certainly always found labels—especially codifications such as

"classicism, "regionalism," and "tropicality"—to be more restrictive than liberating. Rather, as van Schaik rightly assessed, we believe in the "architectural toolkit." Our work is about building on a spatial vocabulary—a language rooted in space, proportion, material, light, and structure. It is the unifying thread weaving through the many commissions that SCDA has realized, in varying types, forms, and locales. It is a belief in a rule-based set of principles or kit of parts that can be deployed and composed.

In this book, we seek to explore our individual spatial vocabulary, particularly as it relates to high-rise residential projects. By extension, we pose a question central to architecture at a larger scale: how can we understand the contemporary fundamentals of high-density residential architecture? Fundamentals, by definition, are also not singular; they are not exclusively regional or global; not classical or modern. They are never restrictive as they are merely a starting point. Architecture fundamentals must be both timeless and contemporary, stable and evolving. Such fundamentals express a belief in the potential of a universal architecture based on humanity rather than formal expression.

Notes

1. Adrian Forty, *Words and Buildings: A Vocabulary of Modern Architecture* (New York: Thames & Hudson, 2000), 256.
2. Aaron Betsky, "The Suspended Architecture of Soo Chan," in *The Architecture of Soo Chan* (Melbourne: Images Publishing, 2004), 8.
3. Leon van Schaik, "Foreword" in *SCDA Architects II* (Melbourne: Images Publishing, 2013), 13.
4. Betsky, 6.
5. van Schaik, 13.

II
Ten Spatial Concepts

The act of self-reflection upon past work remains exceedingly important, not only as a contemplation of one's position within the vocational sphere, but also as a foundation from which to build upon previously established means and methods. Looking back, I shall attempt to define a design methodology in the works of SCDA.

The spatial practice of SCDA refers to the fundamental elements of architecture (light, space, transparency, materiality, and order) and aspires to humanist qualities such as calmness, beauty, and order. Spaces are composed to be experienced sequentially through choreographed processions that recenter and realign the perceptual "axis," terminating in landscaped vistas or open spaces. The approach is phenomenological, and is about the emotional response of the user to the space. The figure of architectural forms, which are often a series of rectangular boxes defined by equally important courts, gardens, and other external spaces, are set against the walled boundaries of a given urban lot. These lots tend to be fairly rectangular, and when they are not, the differences are usually taken up by shrubs, or landscape as poche. This organizational strategy allows for the concept of "inversion," and can be interpreted architecturally as the building and the outdoor court spaces (grounds) being given equal importance and weight, and has been applied to projects such as the Heeren Street House in Malacca, the Fifth Avenue House, and the Sennett House, among others, where the diagram of the expected open spaces (grounds) has been used to generate the building form.

The interstitial spaces between the building and its perimeter boundaries, often created by zoning bylaws as setbacks, are claimed to become defined view courts. Corners of rooms are often cut to destabilize the space, propagating it outwards toward the garden or courts while allowing for possibilities of refocusing the spaces centrifugally toward internal courts in the more urban typologies. Large sliding doors that disappear into pockets blend interior realm with the fully exterior surface.

In the increasingly urbanized suburbs of Asia, there is a need for controlled views to ensure privacy of the occupants and this is manifested in the introduction of small courtyards and light wells within the plans. The incorporation of vernacular features in the early projects relied more on the imagery of the large overhanging hipped roofs of the colonial black and white bungalows. With time, the projects began to evolve into more subtle compositions of spaces based on abstracted forms, and on the circulation patterns of Asian dwellings.

The vocabulary that has been established in our design language allows for typological interpretations of the houses we designed in South Asia. These projects—particularly the residential developments in the tropics—focused on the treatment of "in-between spaces" or the ambiguous boundaries between the inside and outside; a necessary architectural response to the climate of the tropics. The device deployed (the perforated surface, the tectonic screen or lattice of timber, metal, or masonry) is manually or mechanically operated to temper the heat and glare of the sun in the equatorial climate. A staple of the vernacular tropical house, the screen is neither an opaque wall nor a transparent glass partition, yet shares common characteristics with both. An architectural veil that alters the quality of light and shadow, the screen dematerializes surfaces and allows for translucency or opaqueness when strategically lit.

Liberated from notions of representation and the vernacular, the massing and facade is built on archetypal elements, of volume, light, and surface. Walls are treated as distinct planes, compelling a physical separation and material differentiation between intersecting volumes and surfaces. While this vocabulary provides possibilities to re-interpret and transform the spatial essence of a given vernacular, it is also able to incorporate the rudimentary elements of place making through considered interpretation of local craft, culture, and climate.

This process of understanding by rote the basic building blocks of the architecture is not unlike the training in architecture in the Beaux Arts. One must not confuse a consistent design language with a familiar style. I must stress that this approach has not in any way diminished the ability to layer a process and concept-oriented approach with the design practice; while the spirit of the spaces are classical, the details are universally modern.

The commissions of the Lincoln Modern and the Ladyhill in 1999 provided opportunities to adapt elements gleaned from low-rise spatial typologies to contemporary high-rise and multi-unit dwellings. In both projects, spaces are conceived to be plastic and configured to interlock or slide by each other, opening up possibilities of introducing internal lightwells and court spaces in the sky. In the Lincoln Modern, the L-shaped sections of the units interlock and express themselves in the facade. The resultant sky lobbies accompany each three-story interlocking module, which in turn are expressed on the building elevation. These lobbies—essentially triple-height outdoor sky terraces—bring an attitude of tropicality and appurtenant porosity to the high-rise typology.

In the Ladyhill, six internal courtyards—introduced at the center of the plan—become the organizing figurative space and interlock to form an overall rectangular void, with apartment spaces organized around these spatial cores. Allowing daylight to reach the lowest of four stories without the lower apartment being overlooked by upper units, the geometry employs lessons learned from shophouse conversions carried out at 72 and 122 Cairnhill Road (1995) and applies interlocking spatial volumes devised and introduced in the East Coast House (1996) and the Sennett House (1997).

The interior spaces within the projects are a continuation of the architecture while in keeping with a reductivist aesthetic. Here, the process of space-making involves a necessary clarification of structure and construction, expressing said elements as a composition of intersecting volumes, surfaces, and planes. The palette assembles natural, monolithic materials; kept separate between each surface in order to bring clarity to the overall formal composition. The manner of distilling the spatial ideas to their very essence—as dictated by the program—allows the subtleties and tectonics of the materials to express themselves. To transcend utilitarian concerns of program, the interior spaces are designed to achieve tranquility defined by clear spaces, light and composition.

Increasingly, as practice becomes globalized, the applied design vocabulary has to absorb nuance of climate, culture, and place. Working with a clear design language—in what could be diagnosed as the contemporary postmodern zeitgeist—continues to allow for the reconciliation of issues of universality versus regional specificity.

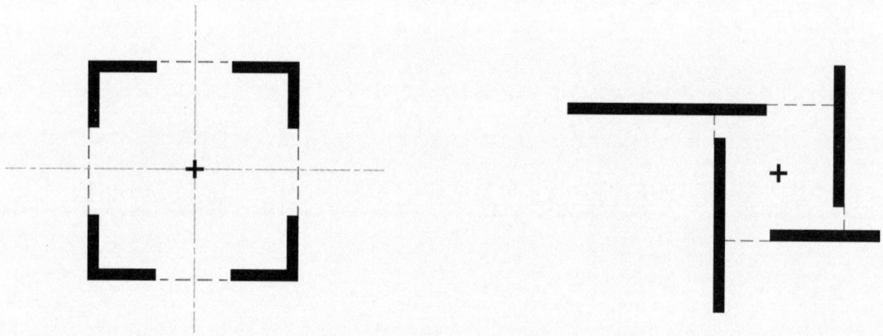

Space and Implied Centers

How to define a center? We do this by dissolving the boundaries of rooms by shifting and overlapping them to find a balance. In our spaces, one can always sense where the center is, even if that space is without a conventional axis and four enclosing walls. Corners are intentionally disintegrated, walls are pulled apart and maintain their autonomy, but one could use objects, landscape or off-center walls to still suggest that there is a center.

One

Centrifugal and Centripetal Spaces

In classical architecture, one is confronted with the problem of rooms and how to arrange them, the classical answer to which is axis and symmetry. However, it is possible to think of architecture outside classical confines, by allowing rooms or spaces to overlap without recourse to a dominant axis. This results in a less axial and dogmatic manner of circulation and spatial flow; one is still able to sense a center, but now there is movement.

Two

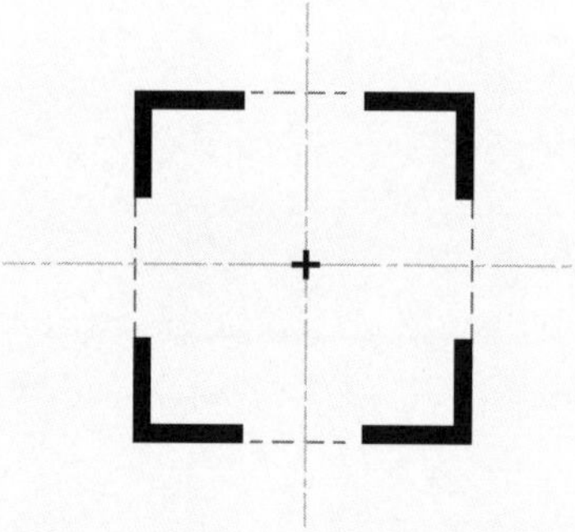

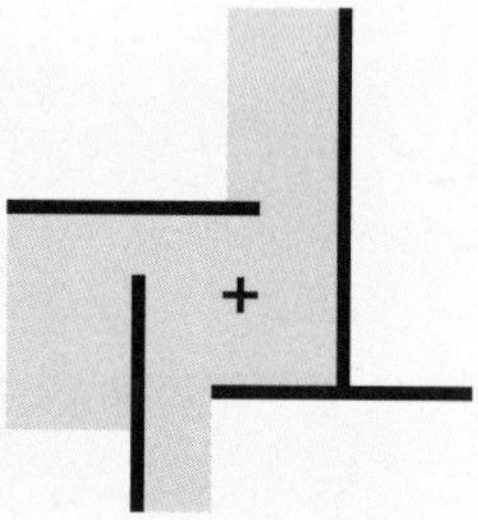

Inside and Outside Spaces

The perceived delineation in so-called western architecture—between built and natural—stands in contrast to tropical vernaculars, where openness is a tested measure to allow natural ventilation. Where western architects have accepted the construction of sealed, weatherproof envelopes, such imperatives apply less in tropical climates. While this achieves greater harmony between inside and out, it has also encouraged an exploration of boundaries, decomposition of the envelope, and the development of an expanded kit of parts—trees, hedge rows, lawns, water bodies or beds of gravel possess an innate ability to encapsulate space and demarcate zones as much as walls, ceilings, and floors. Traditionally deployed in what is objectively outside of architecture's boundaries, used properly they offer a glimpse into an expanded field of architectural endeavors that can exist beyond the confines of interior space.

Three

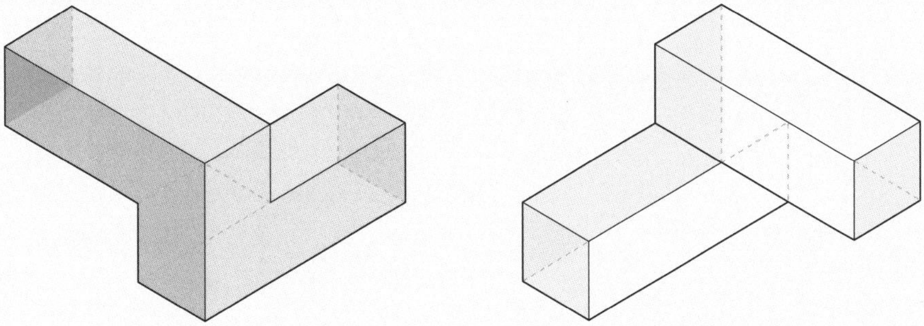

Plastic Space

Spatial plasticity describes the relationship of spaces to each other, vis-à-vis the whole; how spaces overlap with each other, or how they relate in section. It is about how the form of one space is defined by the shape of the space on the other side of a wall. Plastic space evidences the visceral experience of space, manifested in details that reflect a change in function; when the material of a wall transitions into a ceiling, the floor, or the seat of a bench. As in the *raumplan* demonstrated in Adolf Loos's Villa Mueller, plastic space avoids organization in terms of separation by floor, and instead structures space in a sequence of stepped areas, using materiality and detail to heighten the relationships between each area or space, and differentiating volumetric heights and ceiling planes in relation to different functions.

Four

Space and Procession

Perhaps the most fundamental of all architectural elements is the plan. While asked to think spatially at all times, an architect's understanding must come first from learning in two dimensions. Embedded in the plan is immense power of communication. More importantly, it is the first step toward shaping spatial experience.

One must assert that the experience of the third dimension cannot be achieved by standing still. Rather, space can only be truly appreciated by moving through it; to absorb the nuances achieved by changes in volume, light, material, and objects. Similarly, spaces cannot delight the senses by staying stagnant; by paying attention to the transition between spaces we make and allowing them to overlap and flow into one another, they achieve heightened dynamism and tension, and together narrate the story of their architecture.

Five

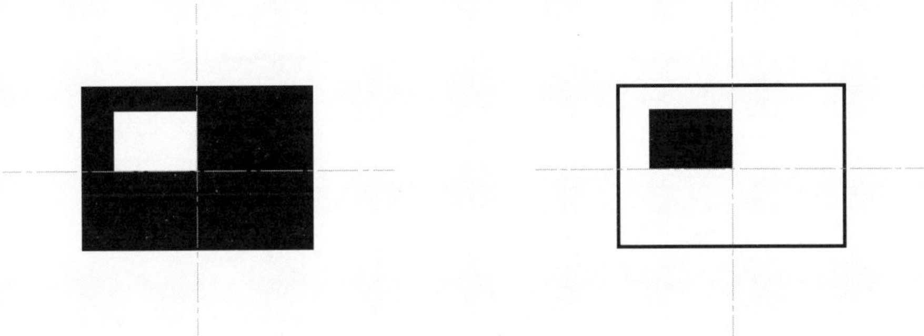

Figure Ground Inversion

The figure ground inversion relates to architecture as it encapsulates space. It is a preference, for one to engage perhaps in a formal dialogue with light, with an emphasis on clarity of form and structure. The figure ground Nolli map of Rome is basically an illustration of the hard line between public and private space, a reading of Rome from the author's viewpoint. It is a matter of perspective. Where one sees the opportunity to puncture the monolithic architectural mass to create courtyards to bring in light and air, another sees the reverse prospect of realizing solids within a void to regulate light and provide shelter.

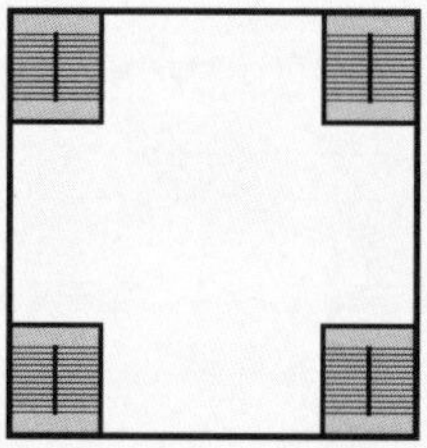

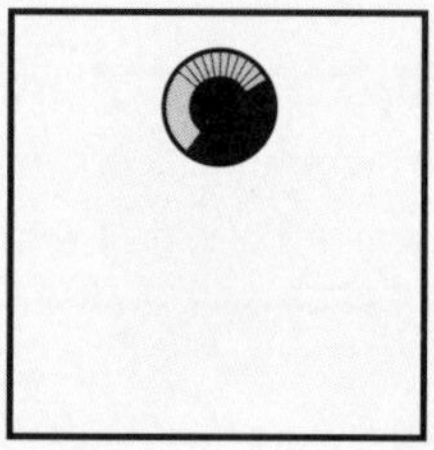

Volumetric Insertion

In architecture, one believes creation must fulfill its function, and be deliberate in its objective. But what of beauty, and delight? Main, served spaces, and auxiliary spaces might be easily separated in any circumstance, but the architect's role is to offer something so intelligent and humanistic that no machine could ever replace what a creative architect could do. An apartment or a service stair need not be hidden behind a homogeneous facade—on the contrary, they can be made to be respectful of their situation in the architecture; they can imbue a space with scale and beauty, a suggestion of movement or lightness, or give a sense of order.

Seven

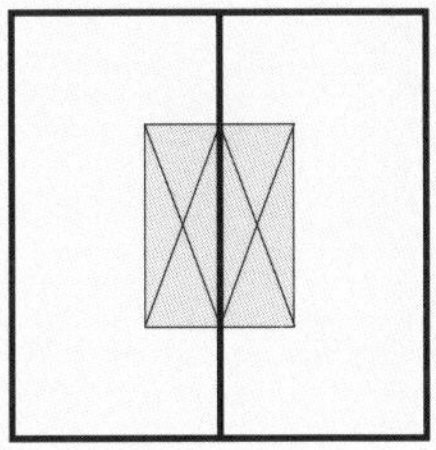

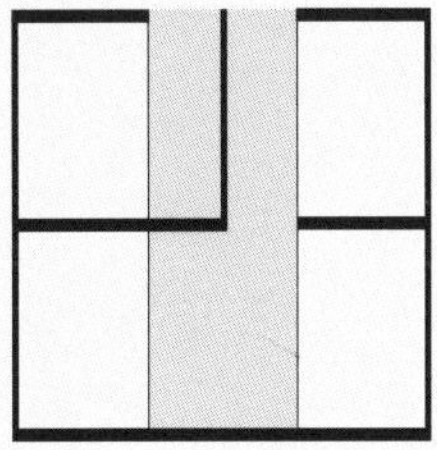

Stacked Courtyards

The void, more often than not, is the result of a subtractive operation performed upon the architectural mass. However, it is also possible to see voids as spaces or volumes that can be aggregated, in a manner one would associate with a brick. The resulting aggregation of differentiated volumes not only enlarges the area of influence of each volume, but allows for a three-dimensional flow of space that functions as connective spatial tissue, while establishing its own recognizable (formal) figure within a building.

In concrete architectural terms, stacked courtyards bring light and air into a deep plan by means of a vertical courtyard; and their spatial variation gives flexibility and adaptability within each architectural parti, along with the ability to bring daylight to almost all spaces.

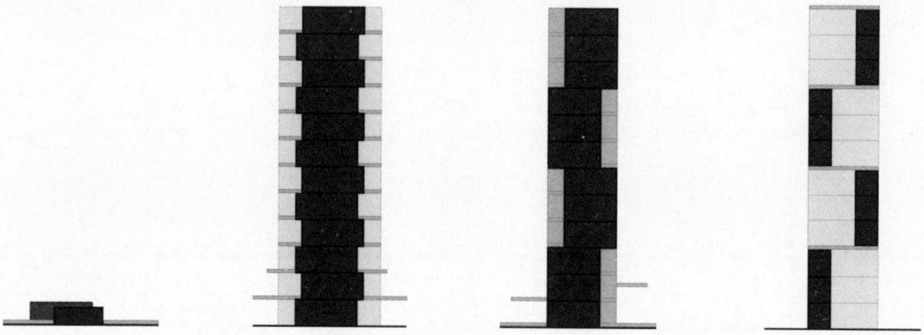

Eight

Landscape and Terraced Spaces

Houses are experiential and ritualistic, a domain in which the encounter with nature and the outdoors has incredible agency to improve quality of life. So why should architecture for density be any different? The challenge with building in density lies not only in the assemblage of discrete domiciles in a finite amount of space, but also in the provision of landscape, without which a space for living is incomplete.

Over the years, the "provision" of said landscaped spaces has evolved for us—from a fundamental consideration into a productive aspect of our vocabulary—resulting in original solutions that have, more often than not, become indispensable ingredients to each architecture.

Nine

Holistic Design

We have striven for the ideals of the *Gesamtkunstwerk* in our work, whenever the opportunity arises. For us, it is not a quest for total control, as much as the chance for holistic execution, from inside to out. Our work on interiors blurs the reading of architecture by addressing light, space, materiality, and internal structure; the focus is not so much on an isolated exterior reading of architecture but also of the holistic experience of the work—inside and out. Few architects have succeeded in both.

Ten

III
Projects One

Architecture must fulfill its purpose, its utilitarian function, and above all must orchestrate the sequential experience of its spaces. The plan, elevation, and volumetric aspects must be developed simultaneously. I believe that distilling things creates clarity.

Each Lincoln Modern residence consists of a single story of bedrooms that expands into a double-height living space. The resultant volumetrically L-shaped apartments can be aggregated, with multiple units stacked vertically to compose a larger architectural volume. While each apartment retains its very own grand double-height space, each interlocks with its adjacent unit to form a more complex whole.

This composition of interlocking units is evident behind a modulated curtain wall, the staggered expression of apartment floor planes subtly interrupting a plane of glass and vertical brise soleils, flanked by deeper recesses which identify the double-height spaces.

The three-story module is repeated on both the east and west elevations, allowing for maximum efficiency by reducing the amount of corridor and lobby areas. As a counterpoint, the southwest corner is reserved for

The Lincoln Modern's composition of
interlocking volumes, lines, and planes at dusk

a horizontally louvered architectural volume that houses the common stair, which is brought to the ground level, terminating in a floating canopy plane that shelters the building's arrival area. Here, linear groupings of trees in varying densities combine with an assortment of walls, floating ceilings, and reflecting pools to create outdoor rooms for amenities while camouflaging vehicular ramps leading to the basement level.

While the exterior detailing emphasizes transparency with the use of glass and anodized curtain walling, double glazing is used with low emissivity glass in conjunction with the brise soleils for climate control—a nod to Le Corbusier's Unité d'Habitation—attached to the floor slabs. In some areas the fins project 1.6 meters in front of the glass facade.

In plan, uninterrupted shear walls form an elongated cruciform, organizing program; rising to house circulation, service shafts and structure; and sliding past the residential volumes to complete an abstract composition of orthogonal lines, planes, and fields of color.

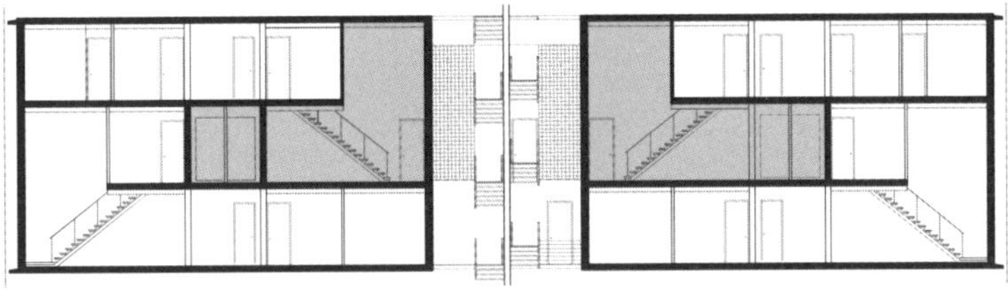

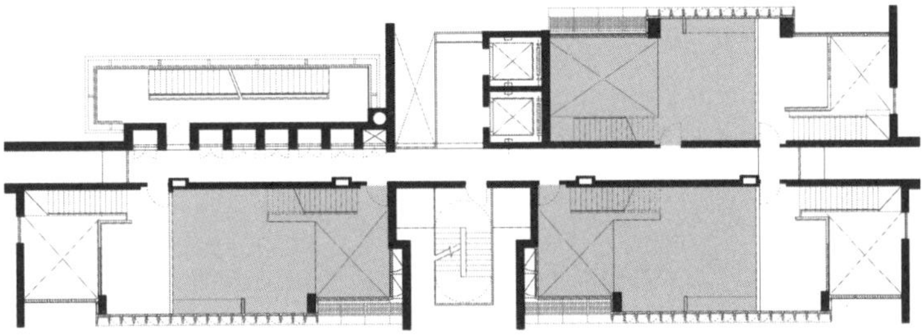

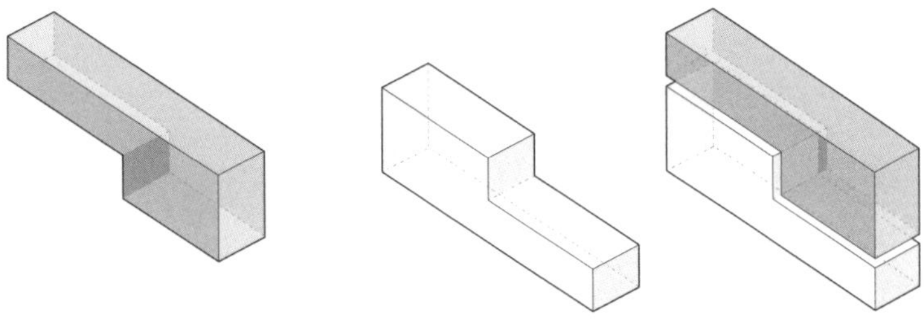

While each apartment retains its own grand double-height space, each interlocks with its adjacent unit to form a more complex whole

The Katana rises 10 stories and consists of 30 interlocking split-level apartments. Situated on Jalan Madge, the site is long and narrow; necessitating a north-south longitudinal orientation with views to the east and west.

As a progression in the study of the Lincoln Modern section interlock, the rotation in the y-axis allows each of a pair of units views to either side. The nature of the interlock is expressed on elevation by exaggerated reveals, highlighting the material changes from aluminum to glass to horizontally clad timber; the expression of floor planes and brise soleil acts as linear counterpoints to the mass of clad, punched volumes.

Interior functions dictate the varying degrees of transparency on the exterior, the interlocking form of the apartments creating a dynamic and visually engaging facade, while on the interior this geometry offers a spatial overlap that redefines the relationships between private and public spaces within individual dwelling units.

A private elevator provides access to the formal entry on the lower floor of each apartment, which also contains the living, dining, and kitchen areas. On entry, residents are gifted generous, unobstructed views to

Interlocking volumes of varying transparency create a dynamic exterior

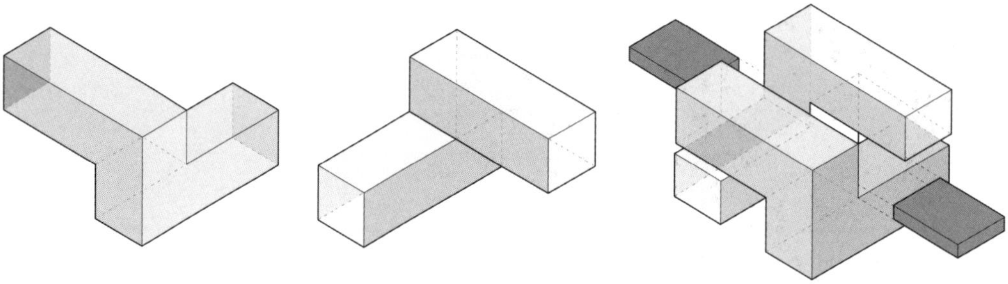

The volumetric interlocking of dwelling units makes possible a spatial overlap, creating units with double exposures on different levels

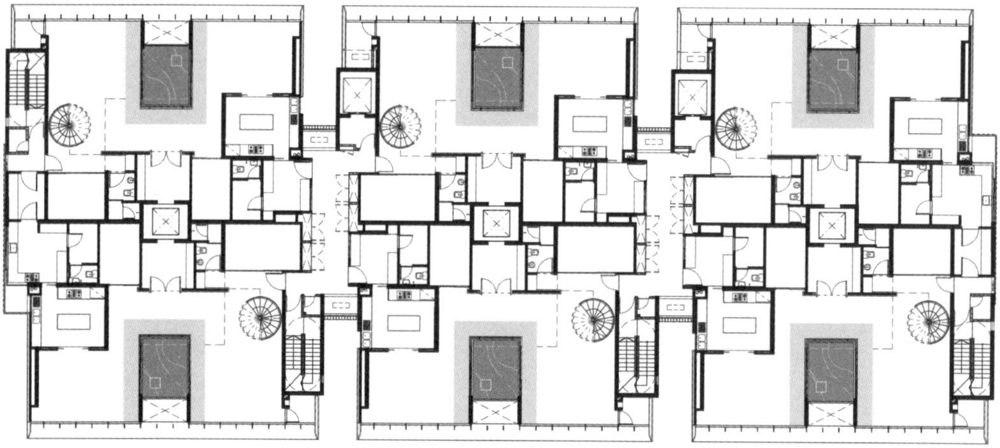

Recesses in the building form are articulated as lightwells and terrace spaces

the east or west. From here, a spiral stair operates as a visual signifier of the double height space, and serves as a pivot point for the interlocking geometry.

While the interlocking typology creates a deep footprint, courtyards are introduced by pulling apartment volumes apart to create pockets of outdoor space, elongating each home's glazed perimeter and thus its exposure to light and air. Seen in totality, the large reveals on each elevation give the building an outward presence of a precise, orthogonal quality.

One KL

Kuala Lumpur, Malaysia, 2004

Dense city centers increasingly face a lack of open space. In this central location in Kuala Lumpur, it was critical to address these concerns. While economic agendas inform development in most cities, the design for this tower attempts to shift this imbalance while fulfilling the program and criteria necessary to sustain such urban entities.

The building rises thirty-five stories tall—thirty-three floors of apartments are set above a base of three levels housing communal and commercial program. The c-shaped plan is located at the perimeter rather than at the center of the site, allowing high density without being overscaled, while avoiding fragmentation of public and amenity spaces.

The residential spaces in the tower are configured to provide inhabitants with a substantial amount of outdoor space. With the building comprised entirely of two-story units, each apartment presented the opportunity to explore interplays of compressed and tall ceiling heights, and the experimentation of spatial overlaps between rooms. From the outside, apartments are expressed as extruded volumes, sliding horizontally along deliberately thickset floor slab planes.

OneKL in the dense urban setting of Kuala Lumpur

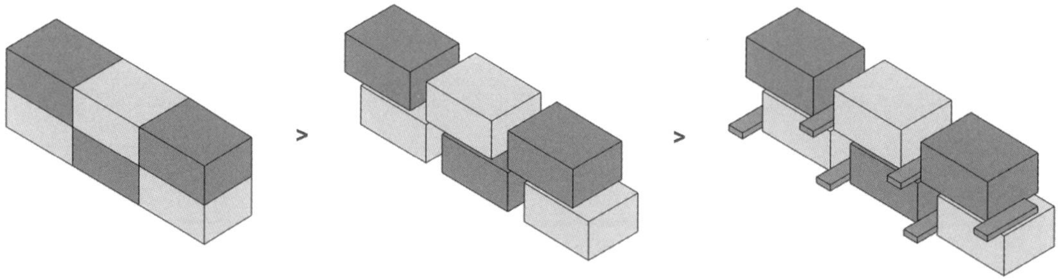

Apartment volumes are pulled apart to reveal in-between spaces used as private pools and terraces

A typical floor plan shows the central screened stair volumes alongside apartment units

By subsequently pulling the apartment volumes apart, spaces are revealed between them that are used as private pools and terraces. The pools are in turn expressed on the elevations of the building through the use of clear glazing at the face of the facade, interrupting each horizontal floor plane with a staggered rhythm. To introduce a sense of scale and movement, sixteen instances of sliding movements occur throughout the 32 stories. The direction of these shifts alternates intermittently in each instance, creating a series of interlocking and overlapping spaces.

Consistent with the vocabulary of shifted program masses within the building's taut, prismatic form, the mouth of the c-shaped plan is resolved by a layering of screens and columns that sheath an entirely exterior common stairway; what is typically an auxiliary space is used to complete the building's extruded mass. Seen from the exterior, the screened stair is expressed as its own vertical volume, while each hinge point of the plan, containing a second stair shaft and circulation landings, is clad in the same anodized aluminum screens. This not only achieves consistency in the tower's articulation, but creates vertical moments of stability to counterpoint the shifted apartment arrangements.

The Marq comprises two twenty-four-story residential towers situated on an expansive landscaped communal area. Where the Lincoln Modern is a composition of volumes and planes, here, a mixture of fine-grained detail and bold, primary gestures is utilized to blend architecture and landscape harmoniously.

Varying apartment modules are subtly expressed while forming a backdrop for swimming pools and balconies, which are articulated as distinct stacks of thick planes that work at the scale of each tower.

The primary tower is built up of a series of large, vertically interlocking four-bedroom apartments, with double-volumed living, dining, and kitchen spaces. Each living area opens out to private terraces where fifteen-meter-long cantilevered swimming pools project out from the building facade. Framed by clear glass, each pool sits within a double-volume space created by flipping the unit above, providing visual continuity from the two-story living and dining areas out to the external deck.

The twin towers present complementary
compositions of the same architectural language

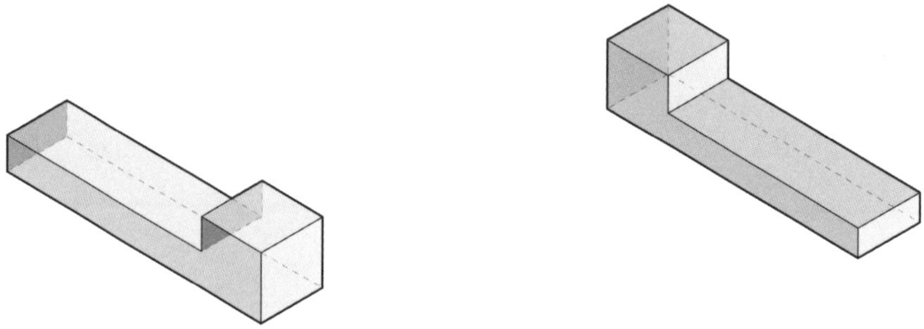

The primary tower consists of a series of large, vertically interlocking four-bedroom apartments

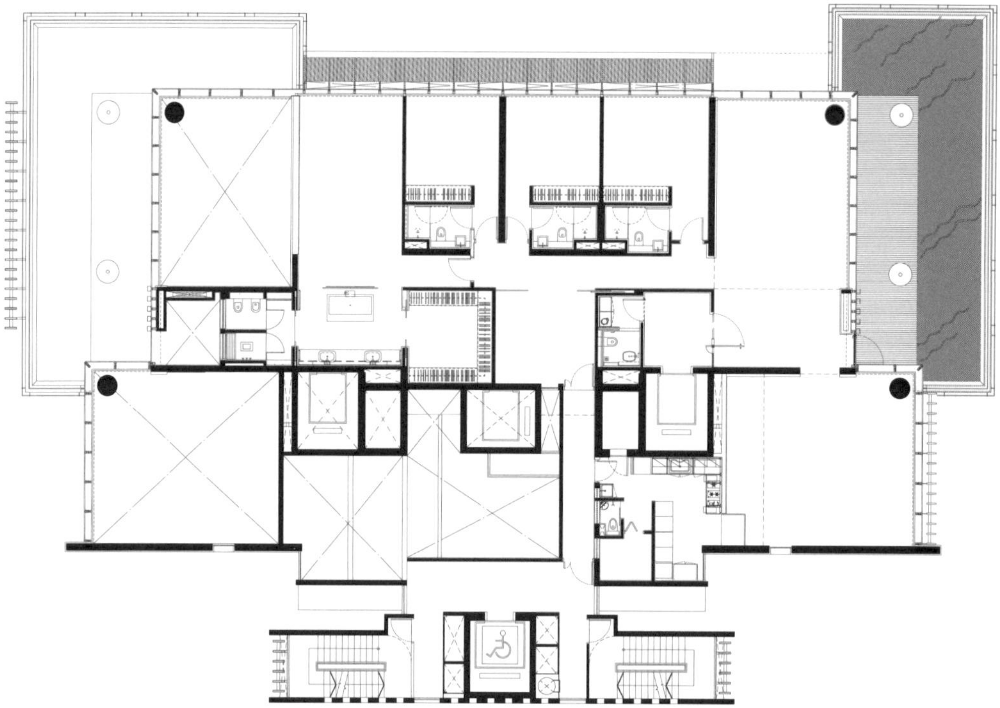

Each living area leads onto a private terrace and cantilevered swimming pool that sits within a double-volume space, created by flipping the apartment volume above

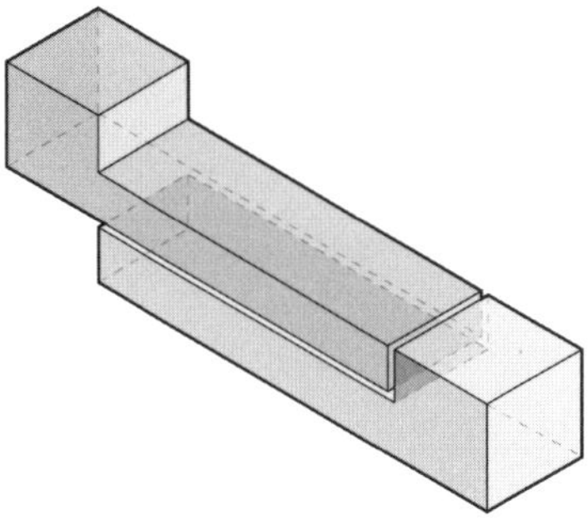

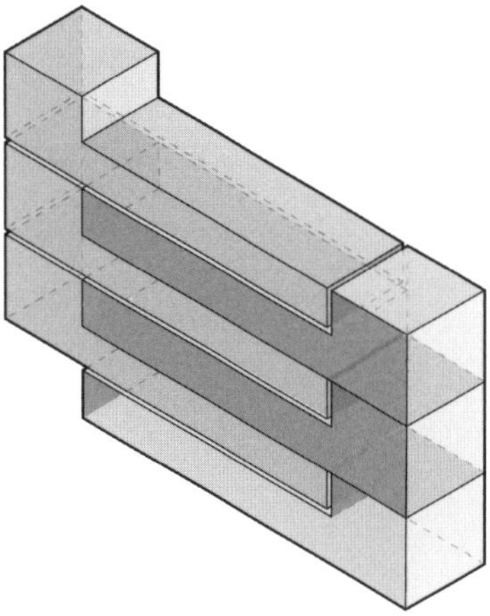

Sitting across the central axis of the site, the secondary tower introduces a three-dimensionally staggered aggregation of interlocked apartments with more modest double-height living areas. Here, the swimming pools are replaced by long balcony spaces that cantilever across the facade, loosely shielding an interior air well that provides a surprising atmosphere of airiness and openness to what appears to be a rather taut glass volume.

Both towers appear as close groupings of boxes that slide past one another, chimeric in the way that symmetries are lost and then found again as one circumnavigates the site. Here, reflective dark-green glass curtain walling combines with an interplay of horizontal and vertical sun-shading louvers and fins that wind and zig-zag across the facade, introducing an intermediate scale to the composition. Elongated perforated profiles, seen in unison with their stiffening struts, produce a screen of remarkable depth that serve as bedroom privacy screens and skin for common vertical circulation, their porosity and resulting play of light and shadow giving the effect of increased layering and depth.

The progression through a series of variegated outdoor spaces is immediately apparent from the moment one enters a large central landscaped courtyard. Surrounded by sloped lawns, one is led up several flights of stairs, before turning off into each residential lobby, or continuing onto a large water court at the end of which sits a sunken pavilion.

Several outdoor rooms, arranged on axis with the primary tower, are sequenced to create spaces of retreat, each with its own particular identity and character. Just next to the water court, an open lawn area provides a nondescript, calm setting for the timber-clad yoga pavilions that surround it.

Moving under a colonnade of trees, one passes a large swimming pool that leads to a two-story clubhouse and gymnasium that look out to the undulating lawns framing the perimeter of the site, with the towers beyond. Conceived as a holistic experience from ground to sky, the project strives to be a cohesion of building, site, and place.

The arrival court

Elongated perforated profiles produce a play of light and shadow, giving the effect of increased layering and depth

The screens provide a layer of privacy to living spaces while dappling the harsh equatorial sunlight

Our answer for new public housing in one of Singapore's oldest estates was a solution embodying three key ideas: housing in a park, connectivity to surroundings, and multi-generational living. The design of SkyTerrace was informed by contemporary socio-cultural considerations and its surrounding urban context. Composed of five towers ranging from 40 to 43 stories, bridged across by a cascade of sky gardens, the buildings are seamlessly connected to the nearby Alexandra Canal Park, part of Singapore's island-wide park connector network.

Expressed as aggregated towers of pre-fabricated boxes in repeating volumetric motifs, each building contains multiple configurations of three-, four-, and five-bedroom units. Emphasizing their individuality—antithetical to public housing's reputation as faceless, stacked boxes—each apartment volume is clarified by the contrast between enclosing precast concrete shells against tinted glazing and dark aluminum paneling. Orienting the fenestrations north-south also offered the best vantage points of the surroundings, while preventing direct solar gain through the glazed sections of the facade.

The five towers of SkyTerrace are bridged across by a series of sky gardens, culminating in a series of terraced spaces at the podium level that connect to Singapore's island-wide park connector network

Each home is accessed from an open air elevator lobby
and is limited to one immediate neighbor—offering a level
of privacy typically seen only in private high-rise apartments

Containing combinations of single-family apartment variations and lofts for the elderly, the module groupings effectually create a vertical multi-generational village, allowing for extended families across generations to occupy interconnected loft units.

Seen in elevation, the volumes of the two-story apartments seem to thrust down and outwards. This near-symmetry is offset by staggering apartment configurations either side of vertical, mesh-skinned common stair wells, which are explicitly pulled apart from the apartment volumes to accentuate their identity as the visual spine of each tower. In plan, the intention behind the separation of the stairwells becomes more than just visual, but demonstrates an efficient solution to establishing maximum exposure to light and air.

As each sky garden connects each pair of towers, social activities and the daily rituals of life are encouraged against a backdrop of rich biodiversity. The gardens, conceived as deep, horizontal vessels with their own volumetric properties, dovetail between the apartment modules to span across from tower to tower, atypical modules that at once counterpoint and unify the stacked volumes in composition.

The pre-fabricated units contain multiple configurations of three-, four-, and five-bedroom units that can be connected to accommodate larger family units

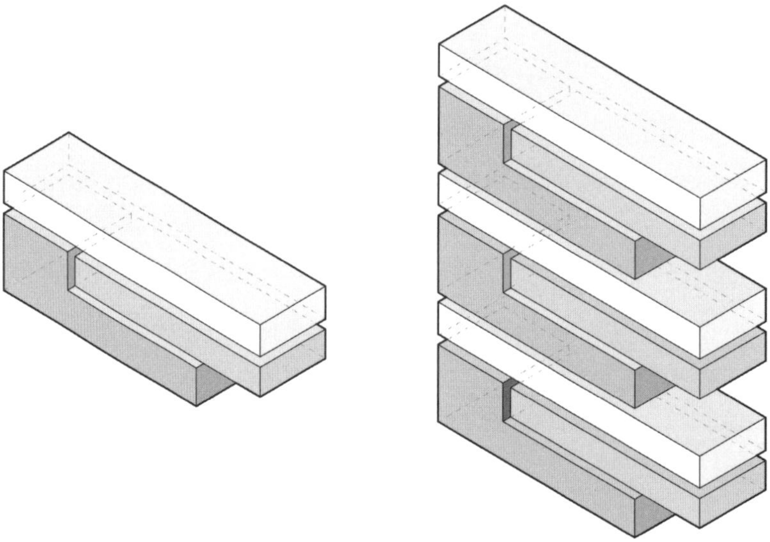

Groups of configurations are then aggregated to form the mass of each tower

Each apartment volume is expressed as a distinct object, contrasting tinted glazing and dark aluminum paneling against the pre-cast concrete shells

A series of lushly planted terraced planes and volumes, interspersed with a distribution of stacked light courts, connect the lower complex of community amenities

As the eye moves down past the levels of green sky gardens to the ground level, horizontal geometries loosen, enclosing a series of open spaces, or outdoor rooms on floors three to six, before dissolving into the ground as a series of thick, terracing, and shifting planar volumes. Interspersed within these planes are a series of stacked light courts, connecting a complex weave of split-level parking, communal roof garden, playgrounds, and gymnasiums to the outdoors while at once enveloping them in vegetation.

To begin the experience from the ground up, a public colonnade that extends uninterrupted from east to west forms the implied center of this village within a park. More enclosed, perpendicular pathways lead to the five points of entry to each tower. Each shaded elevator lobby is shared by just three to four apartments, with each home having just one immediate neighbor—giving an impression of rarity one typically experiences in private high-rises. Finally, within each apartment, the procession ends with floor-to-ceiling windows affording expansive views of the surroundings, light, and air.

Rain trees in the foreground visually blend with the landscaped terraces that envelope the parking garage

The articulated edges of the podium shields a series of meandering pathways connecting the towers to the ground level

The edges of the terraced gardens camouflage program and infrastructure, creating a composition of solids and voids softened by architectural configurations of landscape

Linked to a string of parkways that wind through the city, SkyTerrace could almost be a botanical destination in its own right. Throughout this procession from public realm to private—and vice versa—is the pervasive presence of landscape, in the form of re-planted trees, hedges, hanging foliage, lawns, timber decks, and trellised pergolas—which begin at the ground level, inhabiting the meandering pathways and edges of the three-storied amenity base—and culminate in the publicly accessible sky gardens on the nineteenth and thirty-fourth floors. This landscape conditions the experience of spaces leading to each home, a constant dialogue between being inside and out—simultaneously, inconspicuously, camouflaging the bioswales, rainwater storage tanks, solar arrays, and irrigation systems that quietly ensure its cultivation.

Intended as an identifiable addition to the Orchard Road area, this tower distinguishes itself on the Orchard Road skyline by virtue of its atypical form amid surrounding residential and commercial high-rises. Beginning as a rotated, offset square within a largely square site, the tower's orientation presents a clear attitude toward the corner—with its principal elevations rotated 45 degrees to face onto the busy thoroughfares of Singapore's Orchard and Scotts Roads.

Composed of distinct blocks of vertically stacked apartments, each block is made up of three modules of two interlocking apartment types—a four-bedroom unit with a double-height living space and a three-bedroom unit arranged in a single layer. The modules are arranged vertically to span a total height, or block, of six levels. Clad in bluish glass with concealed mullion details, each block is monolithically glazed. A pair of blocks, set parallel to each other, are then vertically alternated with single, perpendicular blocks that are counterbalanced by a pair of aluminum-clad shear walls.

As the blocks stack, an alternating rhythm of large openings leads the eye to a crown, expressed as a continuous extrusion of the building

The porte cochère and arrival motor court

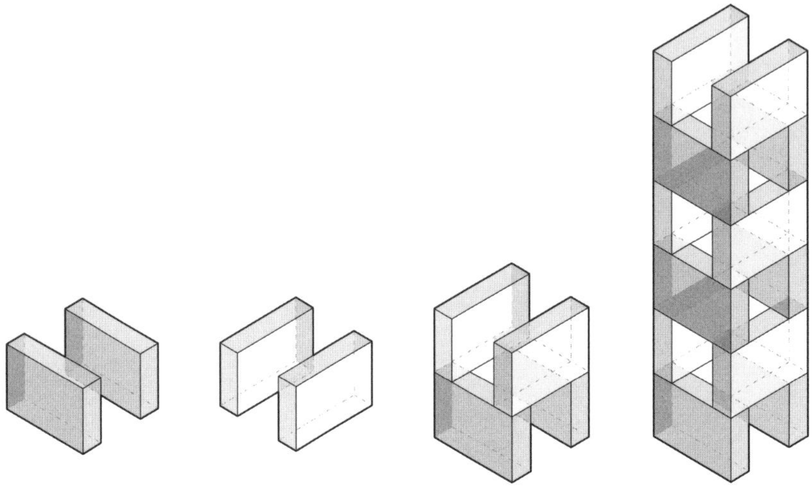

The building is composed of distinct blocks of vertically stacked apartments, creating an alternating rhythm of large openings

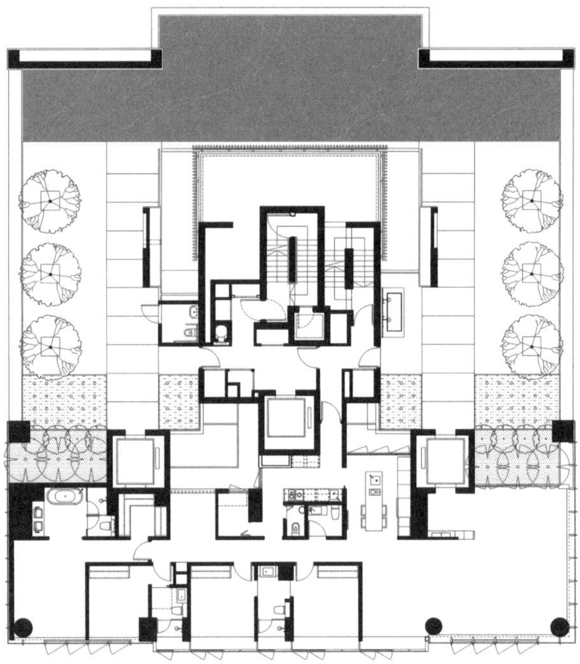

One of five stacked courtyards, which houses a pool area with landscaped outdoor spaces on the twenty-second floor

core. Crucial to the reading of the aggregated blocks is the dematerialization of the core, which is clad in vertical aluminum fins and dark painted stucco.

Nuanced moments introduce deliberate and implicit expression of volumes within the stacked composition, suggesting a secondary scale of architectural rhythms. At the primary floor of each six-story-tall sky garden, a single-storied volume containing front-glazed private outdoor terraces cantilevers out ever so slightly past its single-block parent below, echoing balconies that protrude into the outdoor room of the sky garden. The amenity floors offer a narrative in their own right, housing a pool floor on the twenty-second floor and a gymnasium on the tenth, which, framed by the two uninterrupted shear walls, completes a grand-scaled porte cochère at the arrival motor court.

At the intersections of paired-blocks and single-blocks, each corner is vertically emphasized by subtle jogs of the apartment volumes, their primacy further exaggerated not only by the aforementioned cantilevered amenity floors, but also by the presence of double-height spaces within the apartments at each glazed corner. This interplay between stacked volumetric expressions and horizontal articulations adds complexity to the reading of the tower, which appears different from every angle.

The alternating orientation of the six-level blocks also allows for significant pockets of space that are conceived as six-story-tall sky gardens in the sky—stacked courtyards that literally multiply the lush vegetation of the site up and through the tower. In addition, all units are designed as floor-through units, which allows for natural ventilation regardless of unit size or orientation. This results in a tower of remarkable porosity that one rarely sees in a building of this typology, and also allows the ground plane to be relieved of its typical role of playing host to communal amenity spaces. Here, a more ceremonial, landscaped arrival is achieved, beginning with a grand circular motor court, and ending in generously glassed elevator lobbies that are surrounded by daylight, water, and greenery.

IV
Open Enclosures and Soft Edges

My childhood was spent within the compound of the Khoo Kongsi in Penang, Malaysia, where the spatial characteristics of its verandahs, colonnades, and courtyard were felt but remained intangible, until I learned to "see" them in architecture school.

In fact, a lifetime lived in opposing hemispheres—the Tropics and the West—have led me to realize that these two halves of the world have opposing fundamental interpretations of the encapsulation of space as we know it. This is emphasized in the blurring of boundaries between the perceived realms of interior and exterior. Whereas in the western notion, wild nature is tamed and interior ideals are constructed, in the tropical lexicon, the dichotomy has ceased to exist. Big nature is brought in, almost embraced; the architectural edifice is subsumed by or even servant to a larger universe of space.

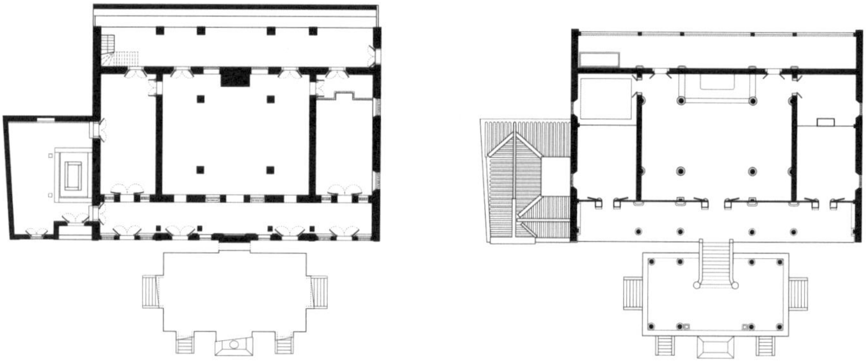

Leong San Tong Khoo Kongsi, floor plans

It would be easy to attribute the difference between perceived boundaries in the East and West to a difference in climate. Certainly, the tropical weather in Singapore affords a certain level of openness, while the harsh winters in a city like New York require protection against extreme weather conditions. But here arises both a polemical challenge and an opportunity—how can we introduce a spatial vocabulary that values a connection to nature and that introduces a sense of fluidity in its enclosure, while acknowledging functional parameters such as those imposed by climate or density?

Voids and Solids

In some of my earliest projects, I was interested in the traditional shophouse, seeking to marry this typology with the courtyard typology and more "classical" elements. The shophouse is a dominant typology in tropical cities like Penang, Singapore, and Malacca, which began as a hybrid of its eponymous uses. Often found lining a busy shop-lined street or harbor front, their open, trade-friendly storefronts conspicuously revealed a series of rooms and courtyards layered deep into the recesses of each city block. A central courtyard separates the front of the house from the service wing in the rear. The courtyards function as wells for light and air. Coupled with screened, punched openings, their phenomenology reveals a compressed, shaded realm punctuated by moments of release.

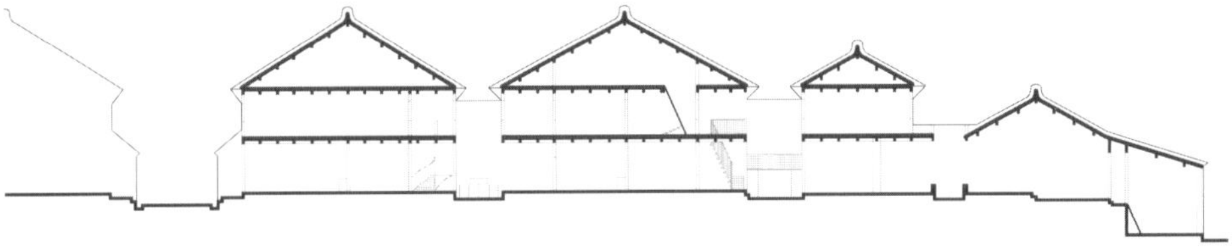

Section of a shophouse in Malacca, Malaysia

In many parts of Singapore, such shophouses are being renovated, keeping the exterior intact while modernizing their interior. One of my first shophouse projects was the conversion of a terrace Peranakan shophouse in Koon Seng Road in Singapore, which I completed for my family in 1999. With a width of only 5 meters, the progression through the house was considered as experienced from a predominantly single perspective. The design was instead sectionally driven. The ubiquitous airwell led to speculation on different ways to utilize this vertical shaft of daylight—something which was further developed in later shophouses we worked on. What became important in these shophouse designs was the understanding of this airwell as a central atrium.

In 1999, we also completed the Heeren House, renovating a 6.1-meter-wide by 68-meter-deep shophouse in the historic Tun Tan Cheng Lock Street (formerly known as Heeren Street) in Malacca, Malaysia. The roof and floors of the original house had collapsed, and the party walls were in danger of caving in. The building's owner wanted to create a meditation center. We proposed that the roof should not be replaced: the building would be left open to the sky and four flat-roofed boxes would hover over the site as an upper level, over a bamboo garden, a performance stage, and a 15-meter pool.

In this project, our exploration of the airwells resulted in an inversion of the voids into solids: the enclosed boxes are distributed over the length of the house, marking a procession through the space much like the airwells in traditional shophouses, but simultaneously referential to a choreographed "itinerary" of architectural moments ideated as Le Corbusier's *promenade architecturale.*

With the envelope of the house dissolved by the absence of the old floor and roof, the party walls of the dilapidated shophouse are the strongest trace of the origin of the building. Evocative of a palimpsest, it is as though history has been etched on their surface. The outline of a staircase, the remnants of low relief plaster panels, the pock-marked blue painted walls, and broken ceramic tiles are a visual testimony of the lives of generations of Chinese immigrants who arrived in Malacca and either made their fortune or died in poverty as indentured labor.

This was not merely a conservation project; it was the first step toward advancing a deliberate approach for such projects. We wanted to present a thoughtful and sustained contrast between new and old, and between the past and the present. The party walls are left as objets trouvés—the

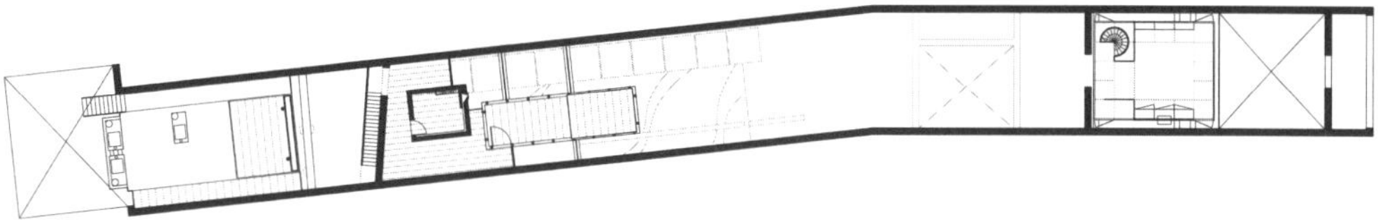

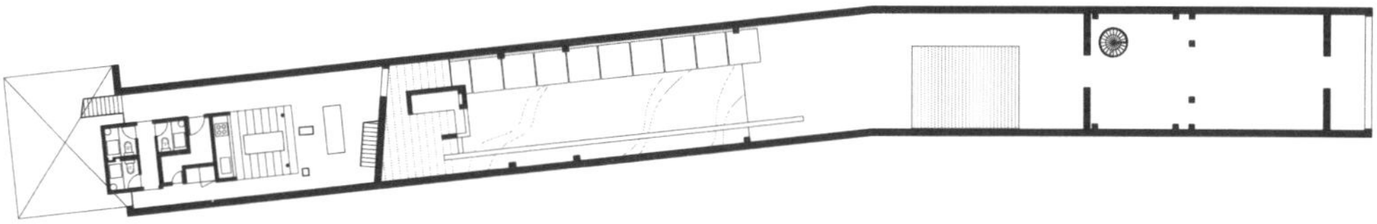

Heeren House, SCDA, 1999

Heeren House, SCDA, 1999

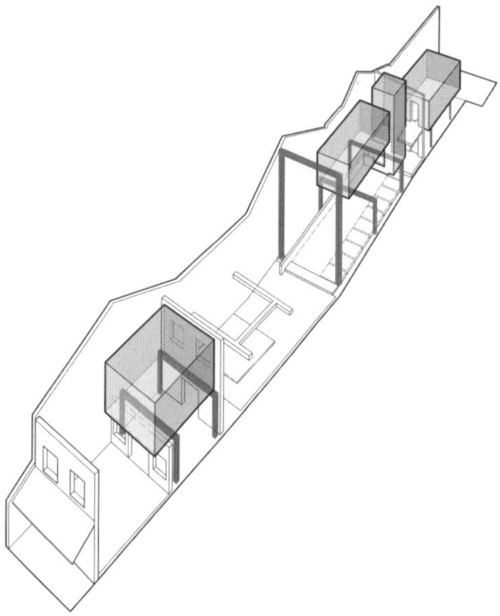

contrasting and minimal intervention of the upper-level boxes heightening awareness of the rich texture and patina of the walls, uncovering memory and meaning in this space for contemplation and meditation.

Overlapping Space

Single-family homes are an optimal canvas for an exploration of ideal spatial environments. Our early houses were influenced by our work on traditional shophouses but their designs also found a productive dialogue partner in western notions of space. The compositional strength of Mies van der Rohe and spatial concepts like Adolf Loos's Raumplan can be discerned in several of our early residences. Projects such as the Walmer Drive House, Sennett House, Fifth Avenue House, Coronation Road West House, and Andrew Road House—built between 1996 and 2000—were thought of as a series of volumetric space, housing programs, voids or courtyards defined by wall planes, sliding screens, and transitional spaces; spaces that sit between interior and exterior. These archetypical elements were composed to blur the distinction between indoors and outdoors.

Projects like the 1996 East Coast House are guided by principles of overlapping space without recourse to a dominant axis. Inside the home, planes, surfaces, voids and light produce multiple spatial experiences within the finite volume. A sunken seating area in the center of the reception space provide an unusual worm's-eye perspective of the house. As one crosses a timber footbridge over a central pool the atrium is revealed in full.

These shifting perspectives also bridge the inside and outside. Moving through the house, one is continually offered glances to the exterior, whether it is to the backyard or a small pocket of open air carved out between the envelope of the house and the property line.

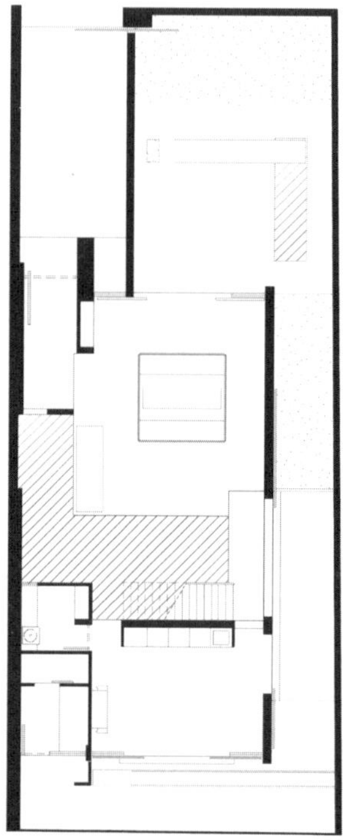

East Coast House, SCDA, ground floor plan and figure ground plan, 1996

In this way, the house avoids typical spatial organization and instead structures space in a sectional sequence. The path through the house is choreographed, orchestrating a rhythm in movement horizontally as well as vertically. Meanwhile, through materiality and detailing, the relationships between each area are heightened. Each planar surface is expressed as a separate body of mass from the next, by means of reveals, cantilevers, and articulated edges, differentiating the height and perceived spatial volume in relation to different uses.

A similar approach can be seen in the Fifth Avenue House from 1998. The house is conceptually a U-shaped plan bisected by a central axis and framing a central courtyard. However, the house guides a shifting path through its spaces. Entering by a gate in the northeast corner of the

property, visitors are confronted by a transverse stone wall. Turning sharply to the left, they encounter a less solid barrier of four vertical granite slabs. Moving around this wall and once again turning sharply, this time to the right, they are recentered on what seems to be the principal axis of the house. Through solid timber doors, the axis is emphasized by the central open-air courtyard and swimming pool. One must circle around the pool, away from the axis and along an arcade, in order to move farther through the house. The symmetry that was initially implied is in fact carefully choreographed as an asymmetrical plan in use.

The Fifth Avenue House makes use of solid stone walls and fragments as well as programmatic elements to direct movement, while in the East Coast House repetitive, successive timber members articulate a screen wall, and in the Coronation Road West House (1998) a latticework of wooden joinery creates a grid, suggesting movement or lack thereof. Such partitions or screens begin to articulate a center through the manner of their deployment, but ultimately, they merely *suggest* volumes of space without ever quite defining them in full; and yet the orchestration of these discrete and suspended elements succeeds in achieving stasis.

Plastic Space

With the ground plane as canvas, one sees how space can be freely manipulated in two dimensions—stretched, compressed, and expanded. When faced with density, one often encounters the need to build vertically; this is where composition and perceived formal relationships between spaces takes precedence—the procession from one volumetric space to the next.

In 1997, we completed the Sennett House. While it is embedded with much of the same spatial language as the single-family homes, this house is designed for a three-generation family. A sister and brother together with their families share the compound with their mother. Replacing the two semi-detached houses previously built on the site, we designed two linear units, mirror images of each other.

Here, our spatial exploration did not merely consider movement through a series of private spaces, but it had to establish a delineation between shared spaces and private areas while allowing for the potential of a third, transitional zone.

The two units are organized around a linear, central courtyard, beginning as a semi-public entry court. As one moves past a screen wall of horizontal slabs of gray granite separated by stainless steel spacers, the role of the forecourt shifts to that of a walled outdoor space, a shared recreation area related to the entrances to the units by openings and thresholds along the way which signal a transition into private space. Slightly elevated above street level, the central courtyard is the principal outdoor space related to the first-story living areas. The two living areas face each other across a central reflecting pool, revealing the daily life of the two families, yet maintaining a distance.

In this multi-generational residential compound, the two units are only 5 meters apart at their closest point, effecting a physical closeness between the twin residences while carefully preserving a sense of privacy for each conjugal family. The Sennett House was designed on a generous site that allowed for transitional zones to mediate the adjacencies between two families and three generations, we have used the same spatial approach to compose living spaces in more concentrated circumstances in our high-rise structures work.

The reality today is that a majority of people lives in a multi-level structure. While it is rare in such circumstances to have direct access to the ground level—where access to natural surroundings and the outdoors traditionally becomes possible—this distinct characteristic offered the opportunity to imagine alternative spaces for living in density, reconnecting high-rise dwelling spaces to the outdoors by introducing blurred boundaries between interior and exterior.

In the late 1990s, we were first faced with negotiating between aims for high quality of living and the economies of high-density housing. New commissions for high-rise apartments provided an occasion to translate our work in low-rise spatial typologies—which celebrated the fluid and open connection to nature—into contemporary multi-unit towers. The opportunity to test the ideas came with the commission of two pivotal projects in 1999, the Lincoln Modern and the Ladyhill. In both projects, spaces are conceived to be plastic and configured to interlock or slide by each other creating pockets of "court spaces in the sky" in an ode to Le Corbusier.

For Le Corbusier, spatial and functional optimization was crucial. The notion of the house as "a machine for living in" was not only limited to single residences, such as Villa Savoye, but should be scalable, applying even to a whole community. This was a concept that he began to explore in the 1920s with sketches for the Immeubles-villas—his response to an urban housing crisis in France. His proposal aimed to provide urban dwellers in high-density housing blocks the same amenities and access to nature as those living along a typical low-density residential road. Each apartment would feel like living in a small house with a garden, except their house would be located above the street.

In these proposals, Le Corbusier focused in particular on how to offer residents a direct connection to nature. He carved out double-height courtyard openings within the facade and volume in which plantings such as full trees could be inserted. Each "terrasse-jardin" was wrapped by an apartment, a complex spatial configuration that was both L-shaped in plan and section.

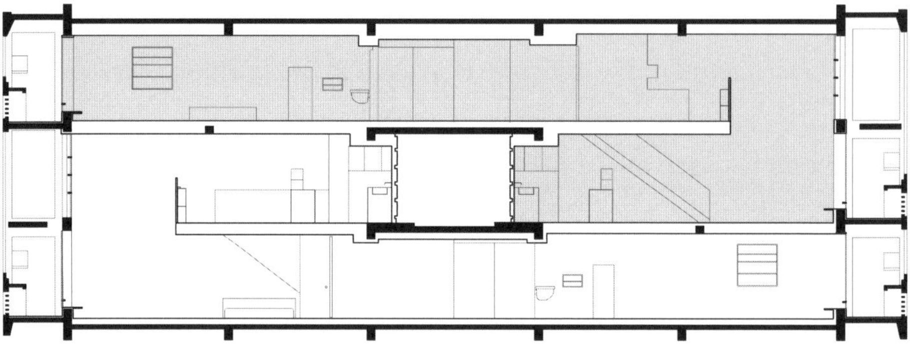

Le Corbusier, Apartment Type E Section, Unité d'Habitation, Marseilles, France, 1952

Le Corbusier's proposals for the Immeubles-villas were never realized, though one sample unit was constructed as the Pavillon de l'Esprit Nouveau, exhibited at the Exposition des Arts Décoratifs in Paris in 1925. However, the same organizational logic is visible in his Unité d'Habitation, which was completed in Marseille in 1952. This building is also best understood through its sectional diagram, which reveals a careful composition of interlocking duplex units that run alongside internal "streets." In this configuration two apartments share three floor levels, allowing for a double height living room in each. The result is a concrete vessel that contains 337 apartments for 1,600 residents, two commercial "streets," a hotel, and a rooftop terrace—a self-contained "city within a city."

Similar spatial relationships are at the core of the Lincoln Modern. However, while in Unité d'Habitation the apartments run across the building, in the Lincoln Modern the section is rotated 90 degrees so that it is evident behind the fixed-glass curtain wall and becomes part of the facade expression. The interlocking module of two apartments is repeated on both the east and west elevations. This strategy allows for maximum efficiency as it reduces the amount of corridor and lobby areas. In the Ladyhill, the six internal courtyards became the organizing figurative space and interlock to form a rectangular volume. The apartment spaces are then organized around this spatial core. The interior spaces within the projects are the continuation of the architecture.

This structural and conceptual strategy has guided many of our residential high-rise projects since the Lincoln Modern and the Ladyhill. Many of our projects feature a similar outward expression of the interior, exercising line, edge, and plane as devices created by shifting interior walls and partitions to suggest volumes that can be inhabited.

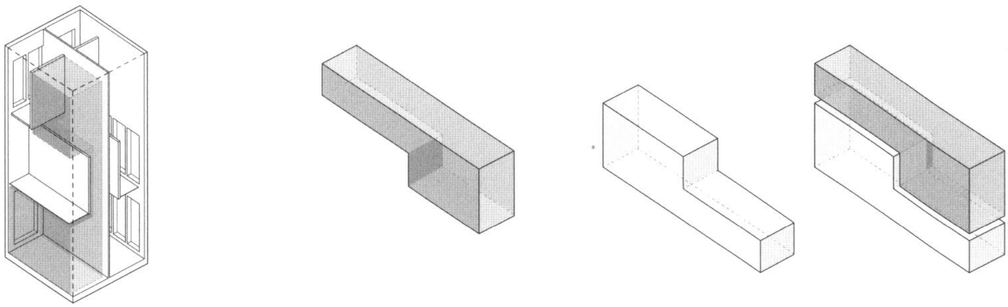

Left, internal light court in a Ladyhill apartment;
Right, repeating three-story modules at Lincoln Modern

In the following projects, spatial plasticity is a common thread. It is a consideration of how spaces are designed in a volumetric sense, and how they may come together to form a whole. We examine this from both a sub-architectural scale of the interior, and the architectural scale of the exterior. While the former suggests a more fleeting and ephemeral composition and encapsulation of space, the latter is more concrete and direct.

Most importantly, spaces are defined as much by their own character as by those that surround them. Our considerations begin with the individual unit: quality of life is the root from which we can slowly expand out to a full building, and subsequently to the scale of a neighborhood and a city.

V
Projects Two

New York's Central Park is a shared exterior; a piece of the city at once framed by the windows of thousands of apartments that surround it, and separated from New Yorkers by layers of air and glass. Central Park South Tower embraces the material substance of the park, collapsing the distance between nature and interior.

Like a two-way mirror, the street frontage presents itself as a glassed vertical plane that is scaled to its neighbors along 59th Street—at once reflecting the park's American Elm trees while allowing a view through to the courtyard inside. This play of transparency and use of foliage starts on the ground floor and brings the eye up to the building's crown, where it joins the rest of the city's famed skyline.

With the tower situated at the south end of the lot, one approaches by foot from the north; past a generous reflecting pool, flanked by immense 36-foot-tall green walls and an enfilade of ash trees. Nearing the tower, subtle shifts in the massing of the building become apparent, producing distinct volumes, each sliced open at their corners to reveal niches for vertical green walls. Inside, a series of smaller lawns and daylit courtyards

The tower as seen from the Pond in Manhattan's Central Park

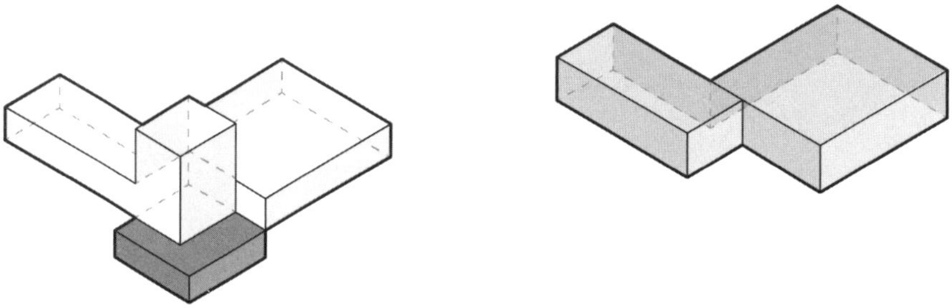

Volumetric diagram illustrating how the three-bedroom apartments wrap around the double-height solarium of the larger four-bedroom apartments below

Shifts in the floor plan produce volumetric readings in the tower massing, bookended by vertical outdoor spaces that further break down the scale of the tower

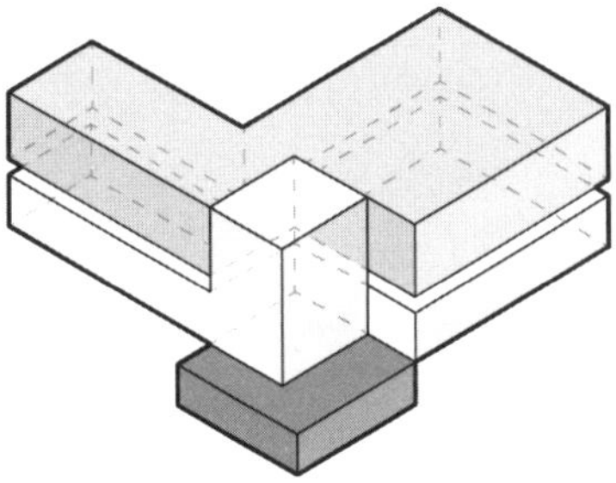

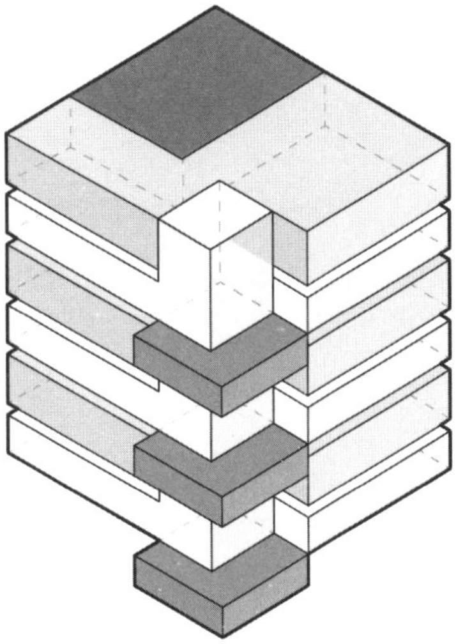

slide and shift around the central core, their presence delineating an expanded garden-realm beyond the lobby's envelope.

Each typical tower floor is shared by two residences, their corners marked by solarium spaces which open up onto outdoor terraces, with the double-height solarium of a four-bedroom apartment cradling a smaller three-bedroom apartment in a now familiar configuration. The neighboring wing features a more straightforward stacking of three-bedroom apartments that similarly introduce a terrace/solarium space at the northeast, albeit staggered in plan to effectuate the appearance of the tower as two tall, thin masses in embrace. Each block of twelve floors—fronting Central Park alongside other comparably sized buildings—is differentiated from the next with a subtle tilt of the facade plane, the terrace spaces alternating their positions between outer and inner outside corners. This divides the height of the 60-foot tower into ten separate volumes that each reflect a distinct part of the Central Park skyline.

Park views are prioritized within each apartment, with main living spaces arranged along the north-facing facade. An end wall is pulled back from the facade line at each alternating stack of solariums, producing vertical slices through each block, incorporating a green wall that spans the height of each block and the depth of each solarium. The perspectival experience of each living space, foregrounded by a green wall set against the foliage of park, produces a visual flattening that transposes the experience of Central Park right into each living room.

In the continental climate of New York, characterized by hot summers and cold winters, the tower design sought the same objectives for integrated green space as in our high-rises in tropical climates. However, instead of a shaded verandah space that wraps the building as in the tropics, here, the transitional solarium layer acts as an inhabitable ballast between interior and exterior environments throughout New York City's four seasons.

Apartment solariums function as a fully transparent thermal buffer that can be used throughout the year

As part of the client's vision of a modern urban village, a city-within-a-city full of greenery, we were tasked with the re-planning of this tower's 417 residential apartments, comprising twenty-five different variations and further divided over six zones.

The master plan imagines a lushly planted, variegated ground plane, above which rise several large towers. Presented with a somewhat bulky massing—a commonplace outcome due to Japan's strict parameters for tower structures—our ambition from the outset was to break down the inherited architectural mass and scale.

The contents of the tower were planned with each apartment zone occupying a quadrant of the tower's deep rectangular plan in pinwheel fashion, typically configured as a vertical stacking of twelve or more floors. Each zone is made distinct; vertically, by the periodic introduction of exaggerated floor planes, and horizontally by deep vertical cuts in the facade. The combined planometric and elevational strategies give the appearance of each zone as its own architectural volume, producing an orthogonal upward torque as the eye moves up to the tower crown. The composition is further accentuated by thin framing bordering each

Seen from the ground plane, the tower appears
as a series of stacked, shifted volumes

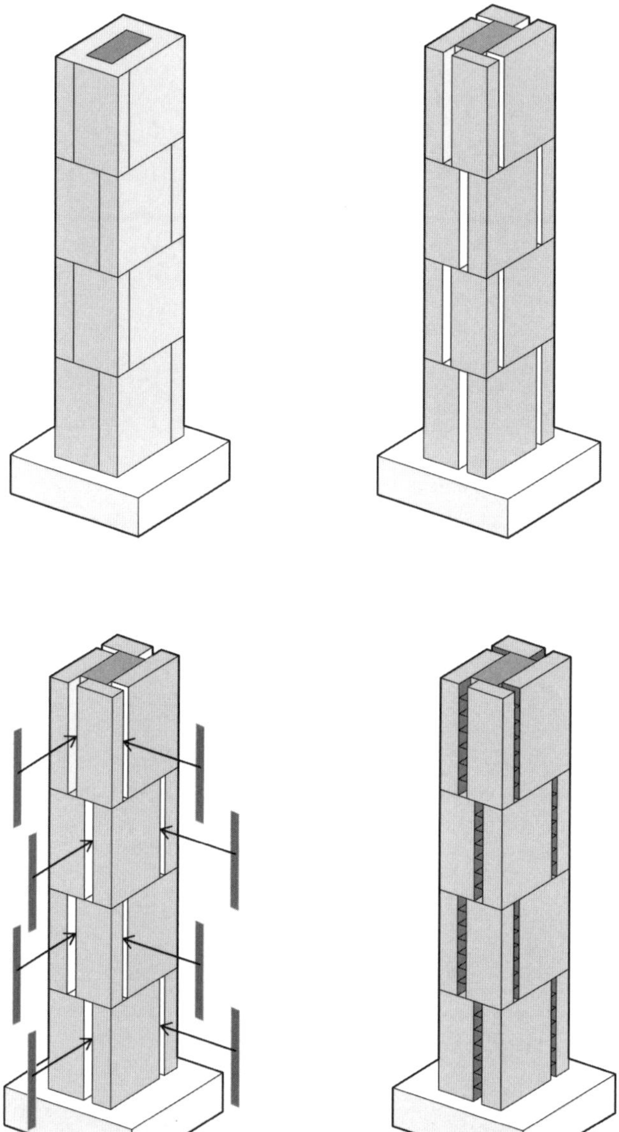

Apartment zones, organized in pinwheel fashion, are made distinct by deep vertical cuts in the facade in which high-ceilinged terraces have been placed

volume or linear element, expressed further by varying extents of projection from the building mass to establish a volumetric hierarchy.

As in the Central Park South Tower, landscape elements intrinsic to the design of each residence are used to collapse the sensory distance between the tower and its surroundings. Here, landscape functions in an expanded capacity, appropriating territories beyond the architecture and delineating a wider realm of experience beyond one's living room. Large double-height balconies inhabit the vertical cuts in the building mass, furnished by living green walls that are enjoyed by both residents and passersby. Considered at the level of the masterplan, the dynamism of the volumetric shifts and corresponding insertions of green walls express an upward thrust of greenery, from public realm to private space. Likewise, the reverse is true: grand-scaled living rooms wrapped in glazing allow for the outdoor space encompassed by the recessed green-bordered terraces to visually extend the experience of space beyond the apartment envelope. This is the first thing one sees upon coming home.

As the herring-bone pattern of the timber terrace floor proceeds continuously into the living spaces, a series of deliberate transitions in the height

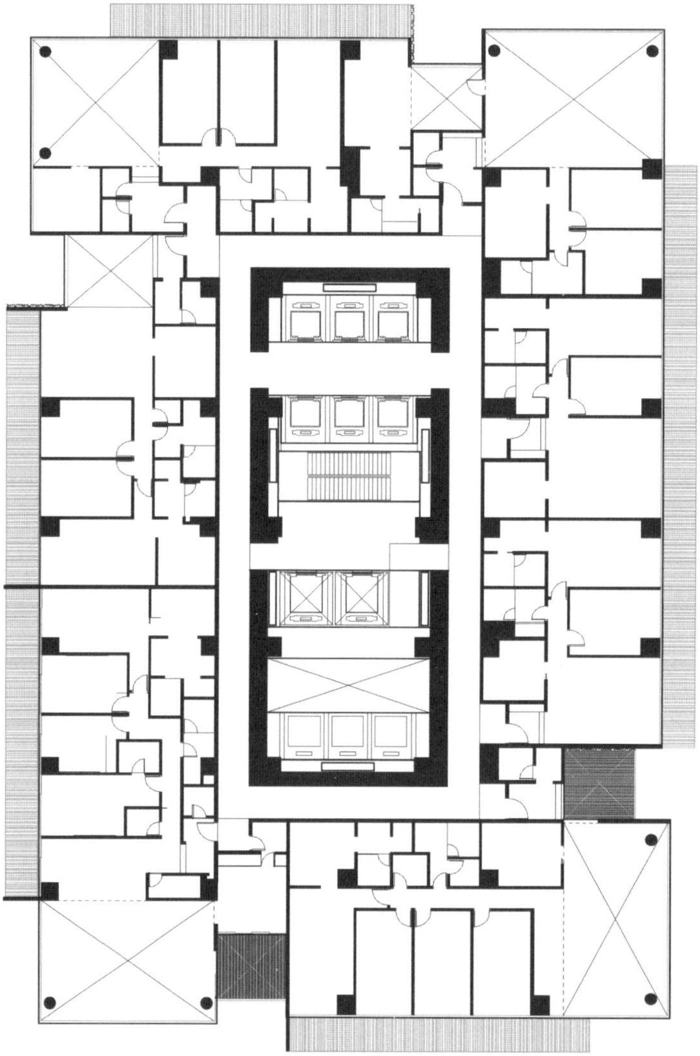

Each apartment is appointed with a series of outdoor terrace spaces that each articulate vertical and horizontal expressions on the architectural exterior

Living areas extensively wrapped in glass allow for the dense urban surroundings to function as a backdrop for everyday living

of the ceiling complements each corresponding room and its hierarchy within each apartment. Subtle variations in the interior material palette also signify specific ambiences and moods that are intended for each space within the residence, in keeping with an overall warmth in tone and expression of texture. Again—this is echoed at the street level, the undersides of terraces and balconies clad in the same shade of timber—a reminder of home on the Tokyo skyline.

Amid the organized chaos of Indonesia's capital city in the district of Kebayoran Baru lies a pristine parcel of greenery; a remnant from the last residential area developed by the Dutch as inspired by Ebenezer Howard's Garden City movement.

At the street level, flights of stairs and ramps gradually ascend to reveal roofed arrival spaces that cascade, through a filter of well-shaded colonnades, into the surrounding landscape. Here, communal amenities such as a gymnasium building and several swimming pools have been set into the earth beneath the elevated horizon line to provide uninterrupted views of the lush site, exploiting the natural 2-meter slope across the existing terrain.

Conceived as a linear plan that meanders through the 3-hectare site, the three forty-story-tall towers rise as vertical expressions of the piano nobile.

A lattice of deep fins and overhanging eaves zig zag across the face of each tower; loosely delineating the interlocking configurations of two-, three-, and four-bedroom apartment volumes on the facade—while providing shaded private outdoor verandah spaces that extend along the

The towers seen in the context of Kebayoran Baru, the planning of which was developed by the Dutch and inspired by the Garden City movement

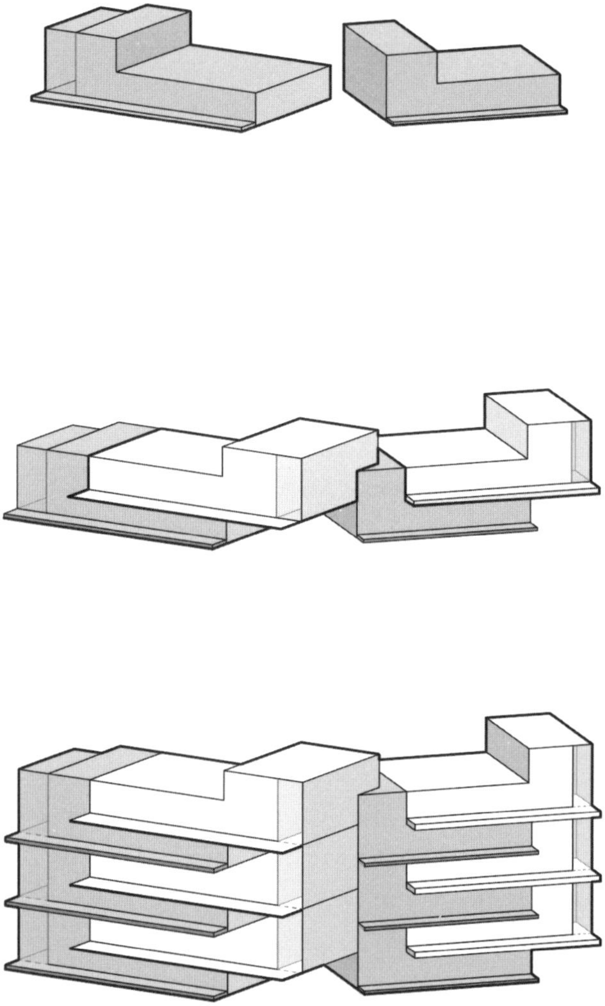

Dwelling volumes are stacked in alternate interlocking configurations of different apartment types, while providing shaded outdoor verandah spaces which extend along the entirety of the building envelopes entirety of the building envelopes. Serving as bookends to the building footprint, living and dining spaces within the three- and four-bedroom residences are attributed double-height ceilings, flowing into equally tall outdoor verandah spaces that optimize exposure to natural light and natural ventilation. These wrap-around verandahs offer residents significant outdoor space, extending the natural environment of the park up the elevation of the tower, while also protecting the units from tropical rainstorms.

The dynamism of the terraced ground level continues into the foundations, where sunken courtyards are carved from the basement parking garage to provide vegetation, natural light, and ventilation into an otherwise inherently uninspiring environment.

The verandahs pay homage to the Dutch Colonial dwelling known as *landhuis* that once dotted the area; colonial country houses that functioned as the beating heart of the Dutch East Indies administration, now Indonesia. Conceived as replicas of Dutch vernacular architecture, later designs incorporated Javanese influences in response to the tropical climate that is hot, humid, and wet.

Reinterpreted in the context of a contemporary high-rise building, the large overhanging roofs of the landhuis reappear now as deep verandah spaces, clad in timber and articulated as crisp, tapered fins with a filigree of aluminum trimming; framing views toward the site's lush greenery and the city beyond.

Natural finishes such as timber and stone are used throughout the towers and the more communally accessed ground level, where cantilevered timber-clad ceilings stretch out into the landscape, while stone columns and floors extend and march past large panes of glazing into the amenity interiors, blurring the boundary between a painstakingly considered interior and the lushly landscaped exterior.

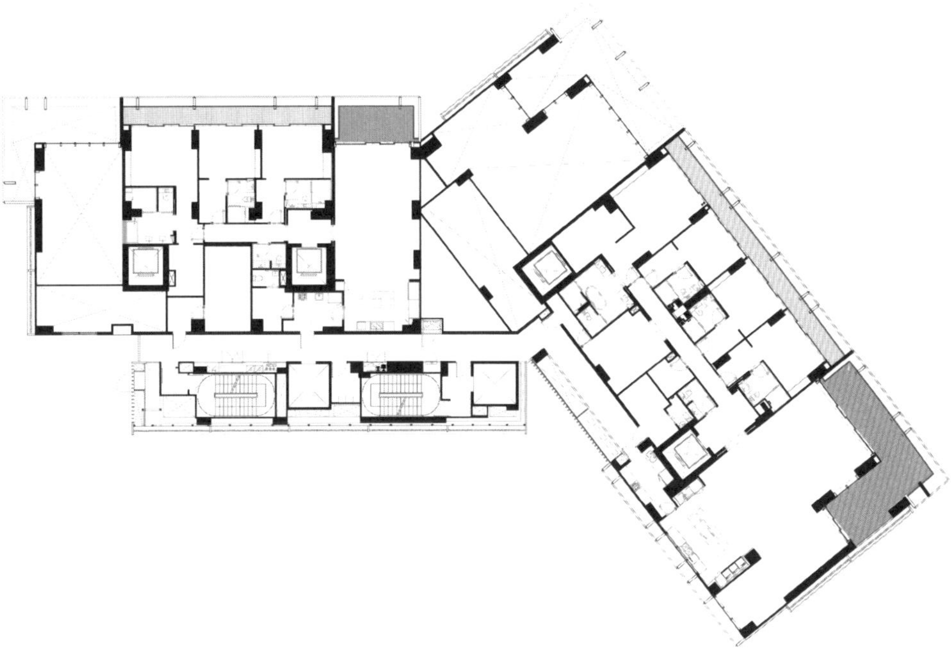

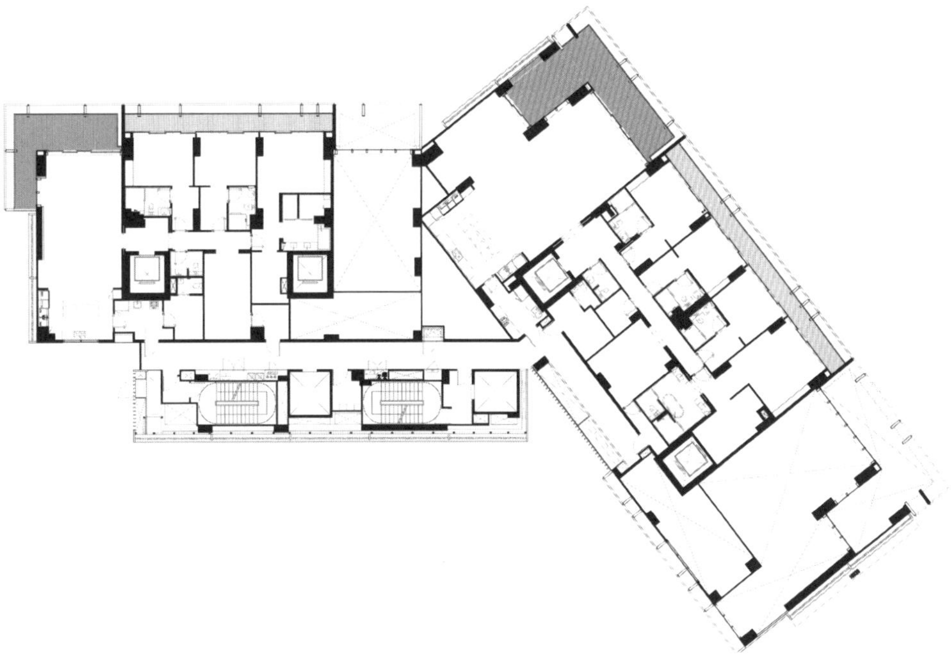

Living and dining spaces are afforded double-height ceilings, bookending the ends of each tower and optimizing exposure to daylight and natural ventilation

Contrary to a great many projects that have benefited from expansive sites allowing standalone structures with 360-degree views, such luxuries are a rarity in Manhattan. For Soori High Line, we were faced with a tight lot facing a narrow Manhattan street. Rising eleven stories, the building creates a clearly articulated street edge by the use of vertical steel fins lined with timber that form a staggered veil in front of large glass facade panels. Double volume living and dining spaces front the primary elevation of the building on 29th Street, giving a grand sense of scale to the building frontage.

Divided into four segments, the third and fifth floors feature four three-bedroom residences with floor-through layouts, allowing precious dual exposure to the north and south. Here, the different spaces within each unit are calibrated to respect spatial hierarchy, providing the primary living areas with double-height ceilings and an abundance of space, while bedrooms and secondary spaces are more intimate in height and scale. Sitting atop each three-bedroom residence is a two-bedroom residence that overlooks the rear terrace spaces below.

Deep recesses in the modulated building facade maintain a consistent street wall datum, while introducing an element of relief

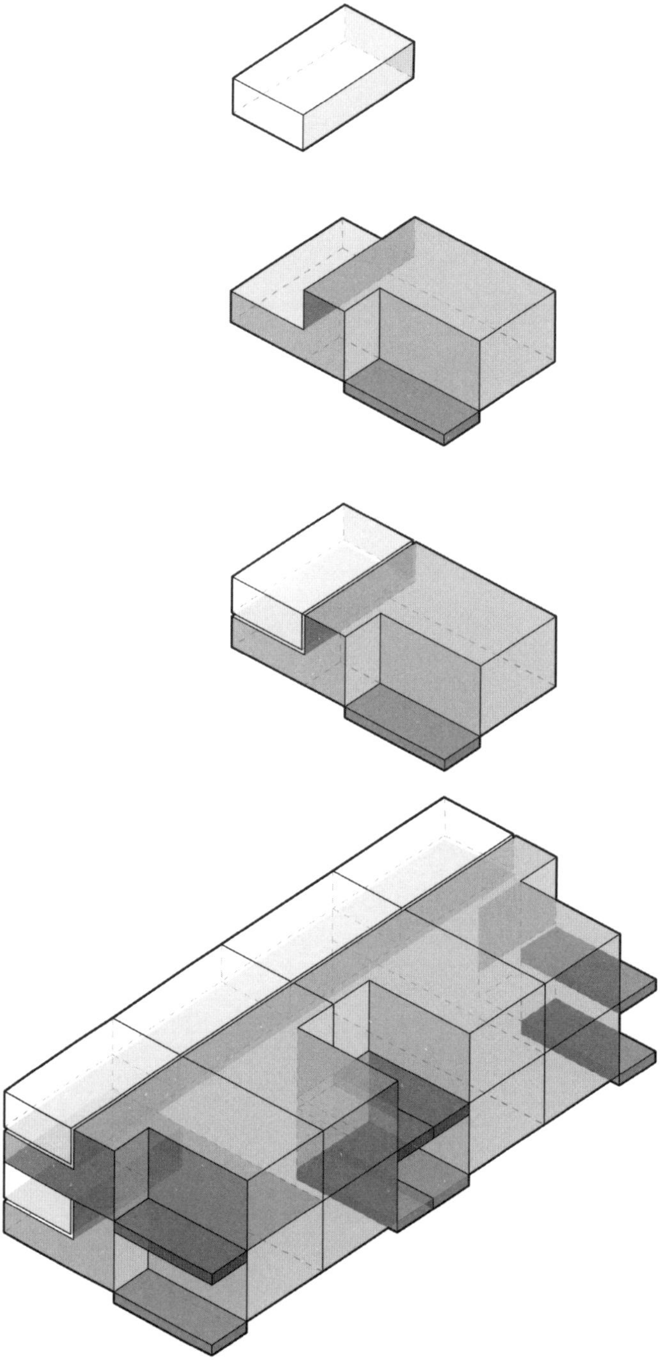

A matrix of volumetrically interlocking units was developed to assemble eight different residence types

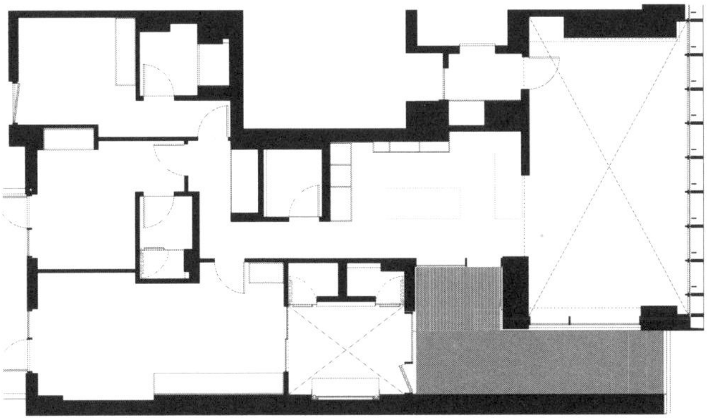

A typical unit with a private swimming pool placed beside double height living spaces

Private swimming pools, set adjacent to each three-bedroom residence's primary living spaces, appear as deep recesses on the building's finned envelope. Each private pool, within a soaring double-height volume, begins at the edge of the primary suite and runs adjacent to the living areas to overlook the street below. Although antithetical to typical New York City developments that prioritize saleable square interior floor area over the provision of outdoor space, this volumetric insertion ensures the immediacy of light, air, and water throughout the apartment. While evident as shaded recesses during the day, the slots in the facade that encompass the pools come alive at dusk, their surfaces animated by a play of water and light.

Contrary to most condominium buildings, there are no "typical" apartments in Soori High Line. With a compact zoning envelope offering only two open elevations, a matrix of modular, volumetrically interlocking units was developed to assemble eight different residence types varying in size, shape, form, and spatial experiences. Largely owing to a minimal reinforced concrete structure that avoided columnar interruptions in each space, the eight different unit types stack in multiple configurations, like a tetris puzzle, to encompass single-, double-, or triple-floor arrangements.

Space within each apartment is approached with a free plan as much as possible. The juxtaposition of a double-height living-dining room with a lower slung kitchen space, for example, leads to a degree of anticipation and tension as the two spaces in proximity to one another produced by their contrast in volume and function, yet are allowed an effortless spatial experience moving from one space to the other. Reiterating this tension is the tall volume inhabited by the swimming pool, which straddles both spaces.

Each bedroom demonstrates procession at an intimate scale; the ceiling is at its lowest on entry and thereafter rises to the greatest possible extent at its heart. In the primary bedrooms, the free plan asserts itself as a provocation to convention. Where typically a door would stand, walls are laid out to informally enclose space; where a door exists, it is made transparent by the use of glass. This is no more apparent than in the three- or five-bedroom pool residences, where slender metal-framed sliding glass doors separate the bedroom proper from the bathroom and the pool

The staggering of floor slabs and vertical aluminum fin expressions
produces an ordered visual dynamism on the street facing facade

beyond. One is able to walk or even gaze from one end of the apartment to the other.

The fire-warmed living rooms and cavernous pool spaces celebrate sight, sound, and texture in a symphony of sensory harmonies that parallel the unique experience of living on a resort. From the silkscreened facade fins and delicate mirror and metal accents; to the leather-wrapped door levers and cerused timber wall panels; the integration of a great many craftspeople, artists, and a plethora of carefully culled raw materials complicit in the making of Soori High Line's architecture and its interiors contribute to the all-encompassing atmosphere within it.

The double-height space of a primary bathroom flows seamlessly to the private pool area outside

Kangqiao Lanxi consists of six residential towers grouped around a central amenity building in a park-like setting. With the entire project comprising three typical apartment types, each residence was designed around a tall living space as a central organizing element.

The smallest three-bedroom residences prioritize a wide living and dining area with a double-height space, while the four-bedroom residences are given the largest double volumes over the living and dining area, and occupy the entire gable end of each tower. The so-called multi-generational family units utilize the tall space as a spatial link between upper and lower floors. These three volumetric units come together as a clustered module that is stacked vertically to constitute the mass of the tower. The facade is a reflection of the diagrammatic aggregation of the tower's units.

While the four-bedroom and double-storied family apartments occupy the same floor, the three-bedroom apartments reside on the next, resulting in a staggered rhythm that skip stops up the building. Slab edges and the delineation between the volumetric units are expressed as tapered, metal-clad edges to enhance this reading of their

The rhythmic repetition of apartment volumes are a reflection
of the aggregation of the towers' apartment units

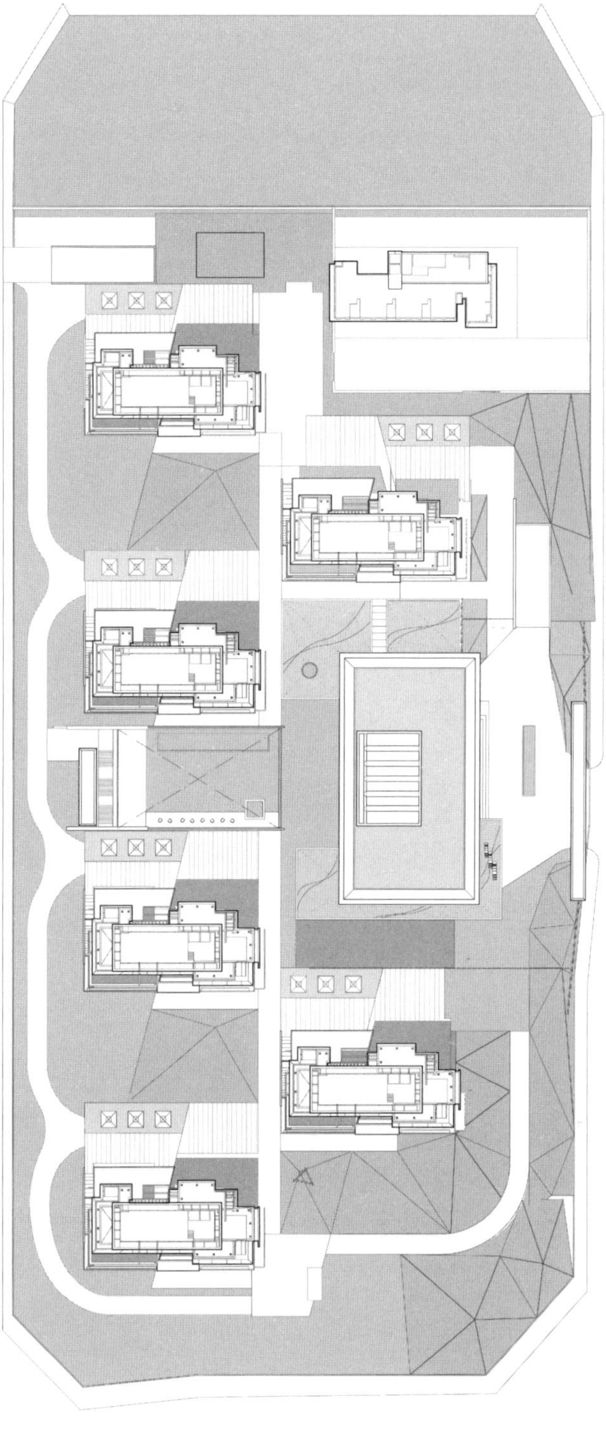

Site plan

A volumetric module consisting of an interlocking stacking of a three-bedroom apartment, seen at top, and two larger four-bedroom residences

Delineation between the volumetric units are expressed as tapered, metal-clad edges to accentuate the overall composition on the building exterior

organization. While bronze cladding adorns the rhythmic vertical stack of L-shaped four-bedrooms on one side, the family units appear as a more direct stacking clad in a dark aluminum on the other. Between them, alternate floors containing the three-bedroom units form an implied central spine to the primary elevation, its glazing continuing above and beyond the adjacent stacks to form a crown for each tower.

Seen from above, a strong axiality of the ground plane belies the asymmetry as delivered by the triangulated lawns and tangential pathways at grade. While the entrance portal appears as if sliding to the left, the doorway of the central amenity building shifts to the right; together suggesting movement about the same central axis that leads one deeper into the plan. Reinforced by a centrally placed

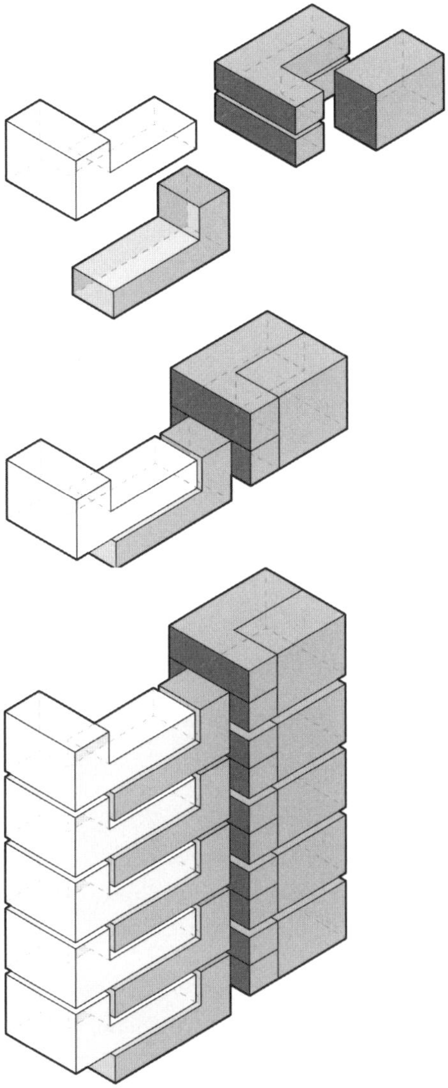

Three volumetric units come together as a clustered module
that stack vertically to constitute the mass of each tower

skylight, this dance around an implied datum is continued with the insertion of a bold sculptural stair that doglegs to shift one's procession down and back toward the entry. Here, the lower level reveals a central sunken courtyard that resolutely reinforces the central axis once again, albeit counterposed by carefully placed planters, sculptures and roof elements that reasserts the pervasive architectural language that continually exercises a controlled oscillation between axis and asymmetry.

Sunken courtyards with strategically choreographed paths
allow for controlled experiences of the constructed landscape

Every new project for us begins with a consideration of the spatial implications and basic rituals of inhabitation. The Tenda represents a new chapter for our practice, with a focus on sustainability, a journey which must begin with the examination of life-sustaining fundamentals.

Conceived as inhabitable off-grid cabins comprising modular kits of parts—designed to be quickly assembled or dismantled—the *tenda* (the Bahasa Indonesia word for "tent") rely on several resource-harvesting systems reliant on periodic daylight and precipitation to realize the vision of a self-sustainable resort on the gently rolling paddy fields of the village Kelating in Bali, Indonesia.

Inspired by the main axes forming the genesis of a traditional Balinese village, which are based on the movement of the sun, the cabins are configured across the site in a linear fashion as to suggest a communal accessway, their angled orientation ensuring unshared views of the surrounding paddy fields. The necklace of cabins culminates in an expressive reception pavilion that will serve as a reception, gathering space, and implied nucleus for the compound.

A fully operational Tenda cabin in Bali, Indonesia

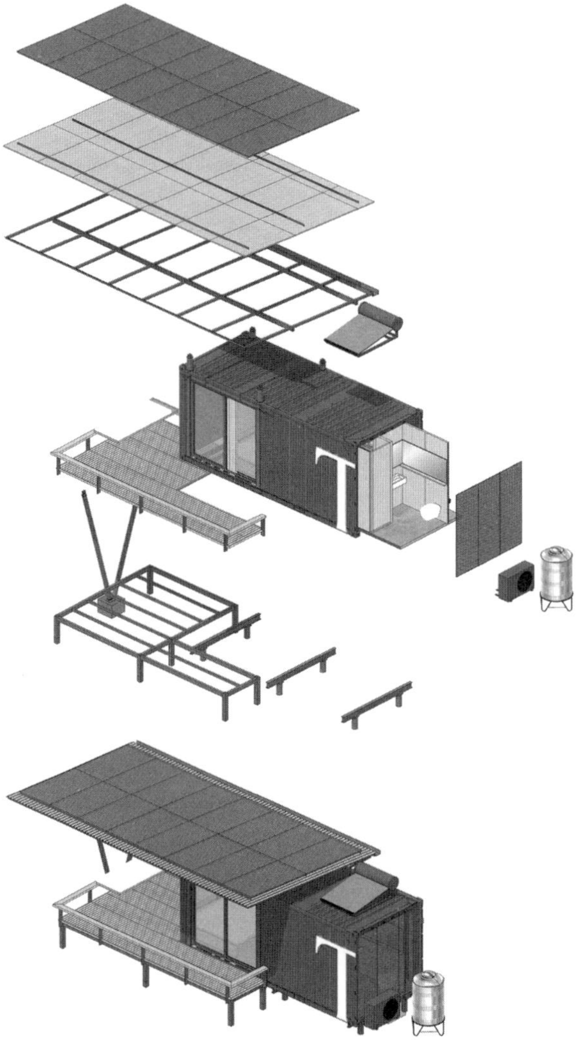

The Tenda are conceived as inhabitable off-grid cabins comprising modular kits of parts, designed to be quickly assembled and disassembled

Importantly, each cabin's primary sheltering unit is housed within a standard 20-foot intermodal shipping container—establishing its apparatus for portability as the very instrument by which it provides shelter. Measuring 20 feet (6.10m) long by 8 feet (2.44m) wide and just 8'-6" (2.59m) tall, the container enclosure and its overhanging veranda roof are supported by in-situ concrete footings and extruded hollow steel members, while responsibly sourced eco-plywood sheaths the small interior lit by LED fixtures. In its modesty, the Tenda presents itself as a universal constant, representing an optimism that one can live at minimum without reliance on modern infrastructure.

The decision made to reuse shipping containers considered the concept of modularity as an efficient means of production, with minimal waste and greater ease of deployment. In essence, what before was a hermetically sealed receptacle for the efficient transportation of commodity has been repurposed as a basic habitat for sleeping, working, and refreshment. Comparatively glassed openings offer privileged panoramic views of the surroundings, giving the effect of being immersed in the rice fields while being completely inside. Although the simple structure of each cabin may contain a single bedroom and bath, the Tenda can be assembled to form different configurations. Intended for portability and deployment in a wide range of destinations, the cabins can also be adapted to suit the climate at hand. Depending on topography and site conditions, one imagines morphed compositions and configurations of tenda to address culture, place, and time.

The contemporary crusade for sustainability has endeavored to maintain an ecological balance by innovating for all its natural needs of power, water, and waste management; shifting toward the harvesting of universally available, renewable resources like the sun, wind, and water. Like the primitive hut that prioritizes the roof to provide the essential need of shelter, each Tenda cabin utilizes its canopy and shell as a substrate for photovoltaic panels, a solar thermal water system, a rainwater harvesting system, and waterless self-composting toilet to support the basic conditions necessary for inhabitation. While the solar panels provide a modest supply of electricity, surface runoff from the roof is collected in a storage tank, filtered, treated, and pumped back into the cabin for domestic use.

A large overhanging roof and a generous deck provide a sheltered outdoor space to appreciate the surrounding rice paddies and distant mountains beyond

A water-free, self-composting toilet ensures minimal maintenance and a periodic supply of fertilizer for farming.

Representing an attitude toward community-building while in harmony with nature, the Tenda will grant visitors access to programs or journeys established by its sister-resort Soori Bali, which offers guests a holistic immersion in local food, culture, and heritage. With an objective to generate a measurable, beneficial social and environmental impact through ecological workshop outreach and material research, the initiative has aspirations to disseminate its message to a wider global audience, with an *existenzminimum* as its foundational vessel that will in time inform evolutions pertinent to conditions of urban density.

The transportable Tenda habitats can be adapted
to absorb nuances of climate and place

VI
On Order

I studied architecture in the 1980s, a period that presented myriad and complex ideologies ranging from the skepticism and irony of postmodernism to the chaos and fragmented nature of deconstructivism and poststructuralism. As a young student grappling with seemingly disparate teachings, I was drawn to classicism for its rule-based approach to architecture. Trained by rote, rigor, discipline, and order, I started my career in Allan Greenberg's office in New Haven.

Order in classical architecture is an assemblage of parts, each subject to an established system of proportions and distinguished by column specificity, pulled together to bring buildings to life that radiate classic beauty and artistic integrity. The city of New Haven was where I found myself routinely constructing architectural columns on paper with the "correct" proportion based on Renaissance treatises, using compasses and French curves. We would discuss how to modify the entasis of a column, or how to exaggerate entablatures to express masculinity in buildings.

It was in 1987 that I first realized that the rule-based classical form was plastic; and was capable of combining beauty and utility, albeit through skilful manipulation. Through classical practice, I had finally reconciled in my mind what had seemed, in academia, the dichotomy between the process-driven modernist idiom and rule-based classical practice. This plasticity of form, underpinned by an underlying structure and language, still holds true to our design process today.

Order continues to play a significant role in SCDA's approach to architectural design—order as organization, order as clarity, order as repetition, order as procession, and order as transition. These are foundational components of the classical language that we have distilled and incorporated into our design vocabulary. At SCDA, a clear and concise design vocabulary provides us with the creative liberty to design for qualities such as serenity and beauty. The phenomenality of space is felt as light enters and animates a room; as materiality, structure, and proportion combine to effectuate a reverberation of the senses. Architectural language—the language of space—speaks through an oscillation between harmony and tension.

Far from its implied rigidity, order can accommodate a phenomenological approach to design when integrated with repetition and procession. It was Vitruvius who described architecture as a combination of "durability, utility, and beauty," the framework for which is established by order.

Order as Organization

Order has always been an underlying organizational principle in our practice and a way to explicitly differentiate between spaces with different programmatic requirements. Programmatic relationships between "servant" and "served" spaces, vis-à-vis Louis Kahn, are defined and organized through the use of elemental shapes such as squares, circles, and cubes; service and function are clearly delineated and expressed using different materials and contrasting volumes. Using order as an organizational tool allows us to indicate where a programmatic mass starts and ends, and provides us with an opportunity to focus on creating an impactful experience of the "served" space.

Order as Clarity

The orthogonal box is arguably the most efficient, economical baseline of architecture, expressing enclosure with inherent familiar structural logic. In our work, order and clarity are achieved by organizing spaces into geometric groups, expressed three-dimensionally using a language of lines, volumes, and planes. The simplicity of this vocabulary allows a high degree of control and can create an organizational hierarchy when afforded thoughtful composition. Order and clarity can be achieved through a common design vocabulary—an architectural "toolkit" that helps drive an idealized geometry that is resolved and can sit as comfortably within a picturesque Arcadian landscape or in a dense urban environment.

Order as Repetition

Repetition can help to organize space, giving it order. In its inception, the classical orders—Doric, Ionic, and Corinthian—were used as basic units of a proportioning system in construction and were deployed in repetition to generate idealized spaces. In a similar manner, each architectural language constantly establishes and hones its own specific rules and systems of proportions that, if expressed correctly, can create an authentic sense of place. Repetition deployed in our work does not express a relationship to symmetry or equilibrium, but is rather a rhythmic repetition of architectural elements framing an underlying compositional datum. This perceived datum allows us to express and highlight certain important programmatic elements to create visual hierarchy and to achieve compositional harmony.

Order as Procession

Procession is a journey, a sequential experience of space that can be rooted in a deep sense of place. A well-choreographed sequence of experiences has the ability to imbue space with a sense of hierarchy and order. Thinking of programmatic space as an episodic experience allows our studio to achieve tension between dualities such as lightness and darkness, and compression and release, while the change of axis provides opportunities to frame internal and external viewpoints.

In our studio, we conceive of our projects in a holistic manner, focusing on the processional experience, seamlessly weaving together the interiors and landscape. A well-choreographed architectural procession can heighten the phenomenological experience of the user and can transcend the space's programmatic requirements.

Order as Transition

Transitional spaces, a subset of the concept of procession, effectuate a more gradual passage from interior to exterior and vice versa. What is typically a boundary between spaces becomes an opportunity to order and heighten the in-between or transitional spaces.

Our interest in transitional spaces has also pushed our practice toward the exploration of the architectural boundary, the decomposition and dissolution of the envelope, and the development of an expanded kit of parts that comprises more than just walls, screens, ceiling, and floors—the physical limits of a building should not be the limits of its architecture.

The perceived delineation between the built and the natural in architecture stands in contrast to the tropical vernacular, where openness is a tested measure to enable natural ventilation. Issues of a pragmatic or climatic nature, often brought about by location and geography, have given rise to balconies, terraces, verandas, loggias, solariums—intrinsic elements of vernacular typologies. The "5-foot way" of traditional straits settlement shophouses or the intricate ironwork balconies of New Orleans, which represent a melding of western architecture and craft in conjunction with the demands of the hot, humid climate of the tropics, best demonstrate the influence of transitional space on architectural form.

It is important to note that my argument for a language-based architecture does not preclude intuitive and process-based design. An argument for rule-based architecture is far from limiting. Rather, it can substitute self-referential wilfulness with logic and clarity. Having an understanding of a common design methodology is important to have in a studio in order to maintain a cohesive design direction. My work has been informed by a conscious distillation of classical and modernist principles, which have contributed to the formation of an increasingly personal architectural vocabulary. When deployed with skill and eloquence, these universal principles of design have the potential to transcend the determinants of site and program, while maintaining the essence of culture and place.

21
16

VII
Soo K. Chan and Leon van Schaik in Conversation

Soo K. Chan This year SCDA celebrates twenty-seven years, and the exploration of spatiality has been a thread that runs through many of our projects, regardless of scale and location. From the very beginning, when I started my company, I was interested in the quality and classical organization of space and volume; how to create a sense of calmness and resolution in a space, but to subvert it by opening up corners and pushing out toward the landscape.

You and I have spoken about spatial thinking on several occasions. It was the subject of your essay for our first book, and you have taught and written about the practice of spatial thinking in your own books.

Leon van Schaik This is an area of focus in the Design Practice Research Program at RMIT (Royal Melbourne Institute of Technology). We have a foundational ideogram for the program that depicts four kinds of scholarship: discovery, where we find new things; integration, where we relate the new things to our existing knowledge; application, when you work out how to do things; and dissemination, which is spreading it.

At Harvard University, a group has been studying creative individuals in every field. They have found that what creative people share is that they come from the margins. The reason this was interesting to the essay I wrote for your previous book was both your background, coming from Penang, and the way you have related to your peers.

For example, while you studied at Washington University and Yale, you worked together with those around you until you had a breakthrough—the moment you knew what your individual approach would be. During your master's program, you were already set on your journey and others perhaps could not recognize it or thought you weren't playing the game. But in fact, you were playing *your* game.

The creative person also seeks recognition from people whose opinion matters to them. I find it quite revealing to think about who you go back to for feedback. Are there any of your peers operating out of Singapore whose opinions matter to you or are you not seeking their insight?

SKC The latter, to be honest, because when I came back to Singapore after studying and working in the United States, I felt informally supported by a group of architects that were not necessarily mainstream. We were a group that was working at the same time and there was a certain clarity in what we were interested in. But we were each working in our own way and interested in our own things. We never got together to discuss a collective approach, but nevertheless, we were grouped in a few early coffee table books. I always felt like an outsider. I had not worked for some of the seminal Singaporean architects like William Lim; instead I was working for Architect 61 and working on projects on my own.

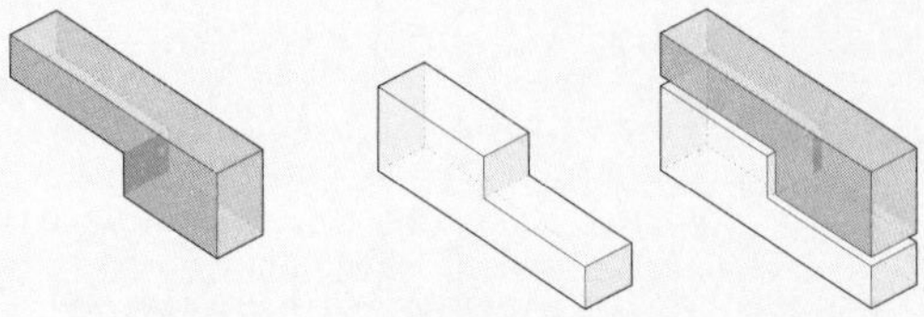

Lincoln Modern

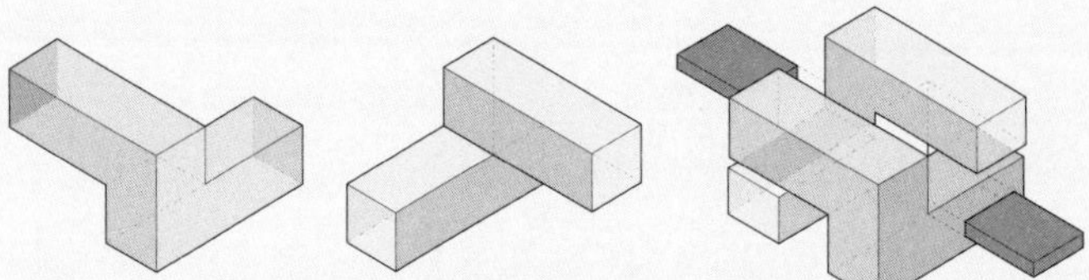

Katana

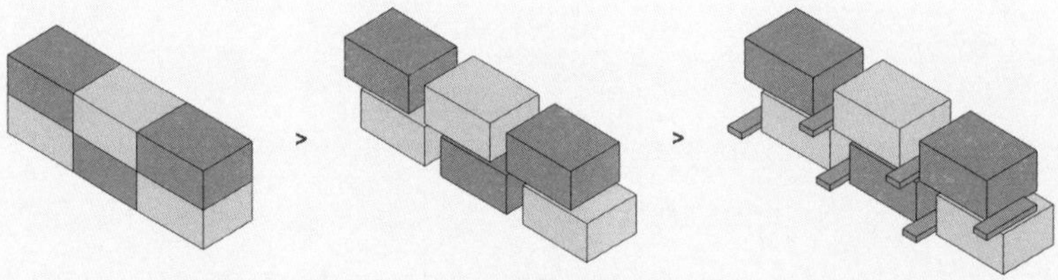

OneKL

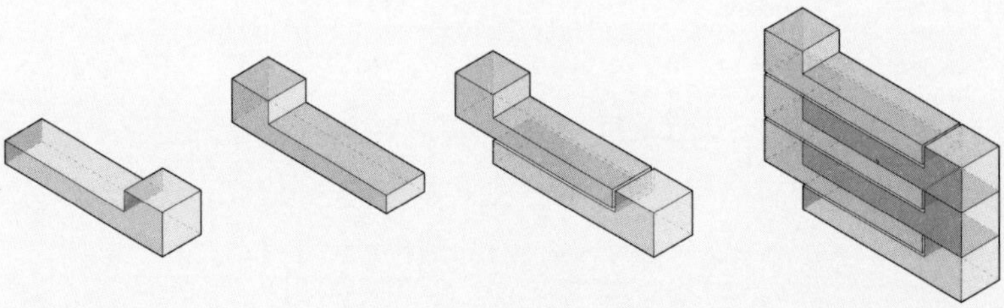

The Marq

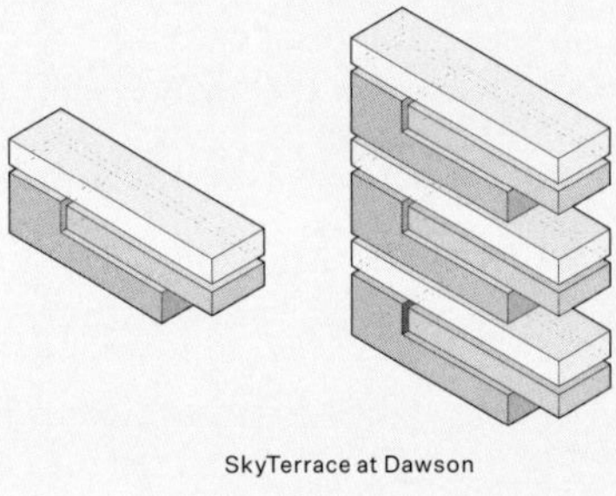

SkyTerrace at Dawson

LvS When you use the word "classical," are you talking about classical Bauhaus modernism?

SKC Yes, but also rule-based traditional classicism, because I was immersed in it for the first years of being a young architect, working for somebody without a computer, like Allan Greenberg. I would have to draw the orders and construct column-based proportions, which I wasn't thrilled about, but I think it served me well. I often look at that as an elemental vocabulary that I can always fall back on.

LvS In that case, you must have noticed a lot of perturbations going on around you at the time; the influence of highly expressive architecture like the Guggenheim Bilbao.

SKC It was not something that I was ever really interested in; I never felt attracted to it. At that time in school, there were different camps. Such expressionism was for the "cool guys" in the studio, while I was with the more "normal" group. Some were strictly Catholic, wearing bow ties, and with architecture that aligned with their traditional religious beliefs. I didn't feel comfortable being in that group either.

LvS This is a very telling piece of your history because, in reading about your experience growing up in Penang, I get the image of you absorbing everything around you. But you engaged your surroundings by abstracting them, and then looking for the essences that lay behind everything. So, instead of getting involved in the decoration, you concentrated on the sound, the texture, and the feel. I can see how, at a time when there were a lot of bow ties about, that the classical Renaissance would have been something to be plundered rather than to be understood.

Yet again, it seems that you were the young boy from Penang in the middle of Washington University and Yale, holding your own ground and saying, "I see what you're all doing, but this is what interests me."

SKC Unconsciously, though I was perhaps more cognizant of it in graduate school. At Yale, I took a studio with Robert Venturi, though he was rarely there because he had just won the National Gallery Sainsbury Wing extension on Trafalgar Square in London. In the studio, we were pushed to design in the manner of Venturi. My project was for a site in Paris, and I wanted to design it in a more traditionally classical way. At the same time, I had just visited an exhibition on the Viennese Secession and I bought books on Otto Wagner. To me, these works were almost Bauhausian, if you looked at the typography, the furniture, the mechanical louvers. I didn't see that as a departure from the Bauhaus. In fact, to me, they were coming from a similar foundation.

When I came back to Singapore, I got a house and the first chair I bought was not a Le Corbusier or Mies van der Rohe chair, but a black velvet chair by Josef Hoffmann. I showed it to all my architecture friends and it was ridiculous to them.

LvS You found a path, in the face of some ridicule.

SKC It makes me fashionable at some points and unfashionable at others. Another great influence for me was Michael Graves, because he was a scavenger of symbols and parts. I bought books on Biedermeier furniture, but rather than reading the history, I was observing the image. Once, I even made an abstracted version of a Biedermeier chair with Michael Graves influences.

These were strong influences on me, but when I returned to Singapore and began my own practice, I was exposed to different references, like the work of Geoffrey Bawa. And increasingly my focus shifted to opening up to the landscape.

LvS I've become fascinated by the process of imitation. Most of the great literature of the world is a reworking of previous great works. There are two ways of looking at other people's work. One is to say, "That's a model of how I think an architect should work. And I'll copy that." The other is to say, "That's interesting. I wonder what the best path through it is, so that I can understand it but not become subsumed by it."

I see this as quite relevant to your work; you ricochet off things. One of the things that happens with the natural history of the creative individual is that—having come from the edge—there's a desire to return to the edge. And that in return, you gain inspiration to go back into the center. Are there moments in your thinking when you use your background, growing up in Penang, as a resource that you bring back into your thinking consciously?

SKC I have thought about that various times. However, to express that spatial experience, it somehow needs to also coincide with the right commission. As our work has become more mainstream and the scale has increased, it has brought opportunity to think spatially in three dimensions. Even in these more commercial projects, we try to create phenomenological moments; to modulate the sensual aspects of feeling the space.

I want to go back to the simpler works as I get older and recollect those strong emotional elements. I'm hoping to go back to Khoo Kongsi and turn fifteen shophouses into something that is based on a memory.

I realize that you often ask architects to be conscious about why they are doing things, to be self-aware and look back to their formative years before they became an architect. Do you think that's more important than their development as an architect?

LvS I think they're equally weighted. You can't become an architect without the formal education and as a practicing architect, you get better and better at what you do by doing it. But the problem in architectural education is that there is no recognition of the fact that every human being has spatial intelligence and spatial memories, and that we build up a mental space.

I believe that architects should know very clearly what their spatial history is. You are very aware of how your background has been instrumental. But the central puzzle to me is that you grew up in a very rich compound, and yet you distilled from it only abstractions. Is that entirely true?

SKC You mean, why didn't I absorb the richer aspects of the iconography of the temple?

LvS You must have absorbed them, but you choose not to use them.

SKC We didn't cherish our own culture and I took it for granted. The temple was very rich, but the actual houses that surround it were much more pared down. That brings up the question: if I could restore them, what would they be on the inside? Would it be a true restoration, keeping it quite minimal, or go a bit more modern?

In a previous essay you wrote about my work, you said that I try to complete things and make them seamless though I had not been confronted with much messiness of context. That is probably a correct reading. Even when building in New York, on a mid-block site next to the High Line, surrounded by warehouses of fish and rooftop water towers, I still tried to create the building as having its own universe.

In order to create a sense of calmness, I carved out a slice, adding a swimming pool; mostly for the sound of the water. Opposite it we placed a gas

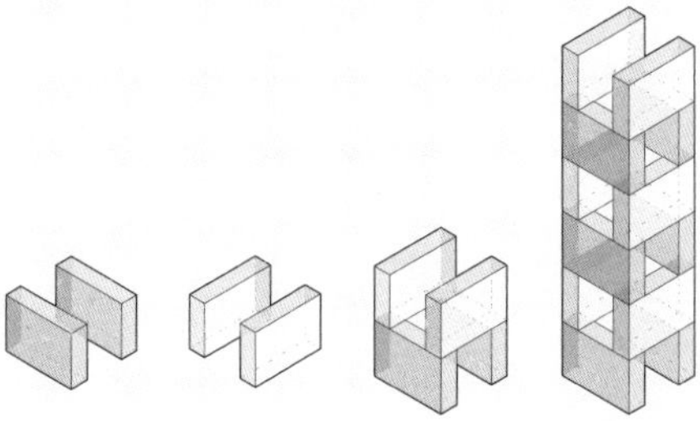

TwentyOne Angullia Park

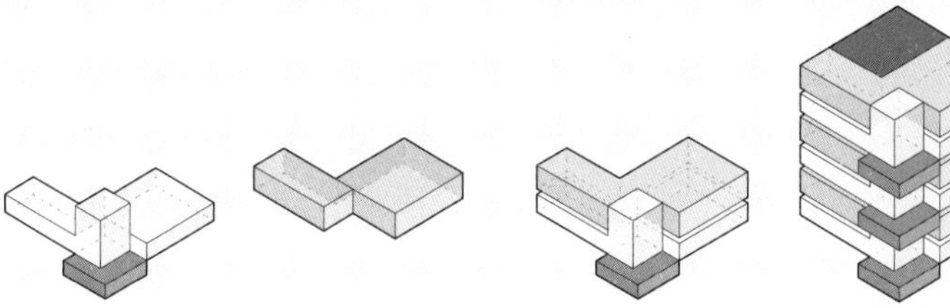

Central Park South Tower

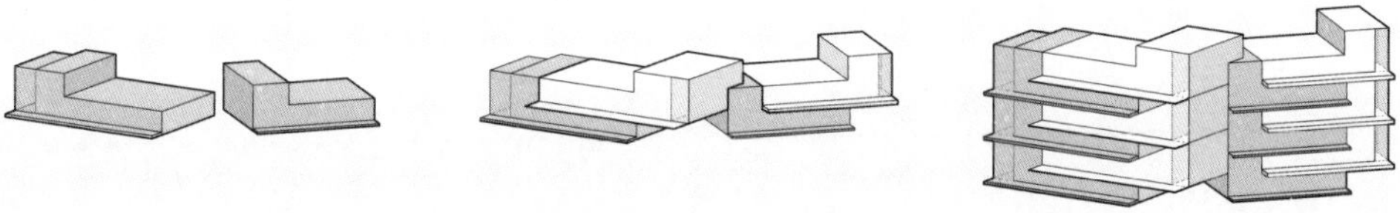

Savyavasa

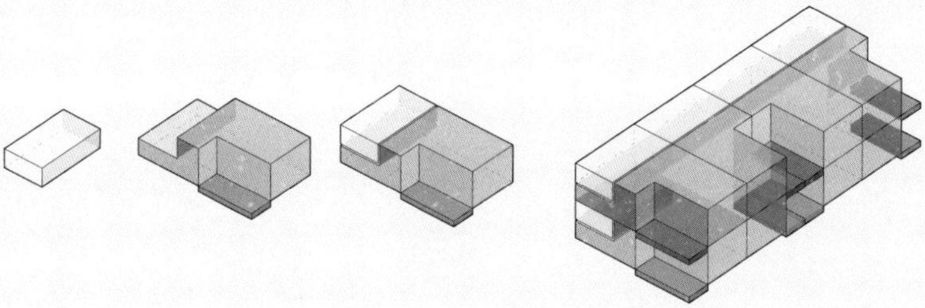

Soori High Line

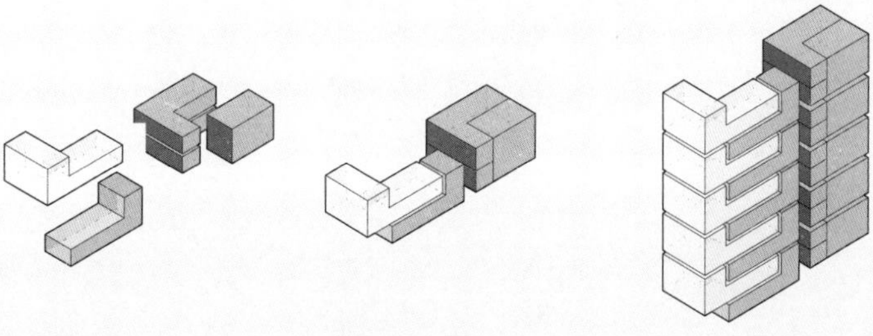

Kangqiao Lanxi

fireplace, so that water and fire are present together. I was trying to create what I thought was essential for the human spirit, especially in the context of Manhattan. When I've thought about it, I realize I want to be in the sacred temple and not in the profane outside.

LvS One of my interests has been the architect John Soane. He was also an idealist, in the sense that he was constantly trying to create ideal situations. But unlike some of his French counterparts, with whom he corresponded, he never got a clean slate. He was always working on alterations and additions. He developed some quite extraordinary ways of dealing with the situation. For example, many of his commissions were infilling courtyards in large buildings. In these contexts, between the building and his inserted design he would create a zone flooded with light to function as a separating buffer that led to his center, where he would do exactly what you've just described, make an ideal space.

SKC It's a challenge to do that when your project is within a dense context, especially for high-rise residential projects. Our site for the Ladyhill, for example, did not have any opportunity for outward views. So, I decided to recreate the internal air well or lightwell that I remember as a child, but spanning three levels. I also started working on a large courtyard.

My early works, before I had the larger commissions, were spatially more pure. I was very taken by transitions, poche, and light coming from the side. But in larger scale works, you're dealing with practicalities of modern construction. So, I became interested in the possibilities within the prescribed 3-meter setback; I tried to control that slice. Everywhere we cut an opening, I created that moment of connection to something outside of the perimeter of the house or building, even for an infill project, where it would be in the form of an air well.

LvS In every project of yours I've visited, I'm immediately aware that you've found ways of doing this. Many of these approaches are quite personal. In the firm, are you very much a sole agent?

SKC A lot of people in the company came their first or second year out of school and have stayed for 20 years—we're lucky to have a core of them. During the pandemic, when we were all working from home, it became especially apparent that there's a strong culture of design that we all understand.

I'm trying to make kit-of-parts that can be used to begin a project at 65 percent. There are some practices that believe that you have to start from scratch with each new project. We're not one of those practices. When working on housing, especially, there are certain modules that we don't need to reinvent. I'd rather focus the energy on spatial organization.

LvS It fits with your idea of rules. A lot of creative people have argued similarly that once you have very firm rules, then you are free to move in unexpected ways. And the notion of starting from scratch seems a myth; you never can start from scratch.

SKC As much as I enjoy rules, I'm simultaneously interested in the meandering procession of a village, figure-ground relationships, aspects of narrow and open, compression and release. In Soori Bali we were able to strongly focus on the spatial sequence. It is an episodic but choreographed journey. I was not able to photograph the building well, perhaps because it is not an iconic structure. But as you walk through, there are iconic moments of spatial experience.

LvS I've been reading a very interesting book called *Stealing from the Saracens* by Diana Darke. She makes the observation that western architecture sees itself coming from Greek and Roman architecture and sees itself as dealing with hierarchies of space.

This can be read through axial ordering; you see defined rooms and containers. Whereas the great architecture of the Middle East is about webs of space. Your design for Soori Bali sounds to me more like the web of space. So, while in your work I see ideal spaces, I also see the web of space.

SKC I'm interested in a processional route that's very direct, but also in switching directions, which is much more eastern. I'm a product of both areas; having had the benefit of looking at some western paradigms and not understanding my own eastern roots because I'm not educated to be able to access it. There lies the contradiction. That's why I always argue for universality in architecture. For me, it is important to organize space in terms of transitions, light, and shadow.

That also means going back to understanding what works and what doesn't. What's a good proportion for an air well or what's an air well that makes people deliberately uncomfortable?

LvS One of the things I'm always doing is counting dimensions. How many paces in this room? Some of the most powerful spaces are the smallest ones. John Soane's morning room was only 3 meters by 3 meters, and yet the entire museum circles or pivots around this tiny space. I see that pivoting going on in your work as well. When we say web, it can perhaps sound as if everything spreads equally in all directions, but that's not what happens—you're constantly pivoting.

SKC At Yale, I remember taking two photography classes. I would take pictures of oil drums, barbed wire, and other very industrial things. And then the critics would say, "No matter what pictures you are taking, it has a nice radiance and beauty in it. It doesn't show the aggressive nature of that space."

LvS You find the beauty wherever you look. Within these stories, I think you're beginning to explain what it is that you're actually looking for in the ideals. You've looked for the essentials, whether it's tactile or visual, or even the touch and the sound of rain. In your photography courses, as you've just said, you found the essences of things. While you have a desire to put people into an ideal, calm situation, your focus is not merely on these singular moments, but on the web of space that leads to them. Surrounding the large, beautiful spaces are nugget points where you feel the space compress.

SKC I think that's a perfect summary to end on. I feel like we've finished a very good therapy session on architecture, and I feel rejuvenated.

Acknowledgments

This book would not have been possible without the participation and insight of several key individuals.

My first words of appreciation and thanks must be to Julia van den Hout and Jia-Jun Yeo for their role in helping to structure, edit, and put on paper my various thoughts on this topic. Julia has been my architectural therapist over the last two and a half years, acting as a sounding board and translating into words my ideas. Jia-Jun has been an integral part of SCDA in New York, and with his insight on my work he has organized, structured, and kept to schedule the production of this book. Both Julia and Jia-Jun sought to keep the process going forward in spite of my many daily distractions. My gratitude extends to Gordon Goff, the publisher of ORO, who believed in the premise of the book and offered to publish and distribute it. Through Gordon, I was introduced to Julia and Luke Bulman. Thanks to Luke who gave form and shape to the text and images through his sensitive book design. My sincere appreciation to all the photographers whose work is featured in this book, in particular Aaron Pocock, who have beautifully documented all the works of SCDA through the years.

Special thanks to Professor Leonardus van Schaik, a keen observer of my work, who had published critiques in the introductions to my two earlier monographs. Our recent conversations, transcribed in this book, were a journey of self-discovery, tracing my work to my early formative childhood years.

Special thanks also to Vladimir Belogolovsky with whom I have had sustained conversations about my work through interviews we have published in recent years. My appreciation goes to Sara Abd Rabbo, Anna Kwon, and Victoria Lee, for helping to gather and organize the necessary materials for the book.

I am much indebted to the directors, associates, and staff of SCDA for their dedication, effort, and enthusiasm without which the many projects featured through the years would not have been realized.

To all my sons, whose love of life and the Arts motivates me to create.

Finally, I owe a debt of gratitude to my wife Ling who has been my bedrock. Her love and support all through these years continue to inspire.

With appreciation,

Soo K. Chan

With Reference
SCDA—Notions of Space

ORO Editions
Publishers of Architecture, Art, and Design
Gordon Goff: Publisher

www.oroeditions.com
info@oroeditions.com

Published by ORO Editions

Author: Soo K. Chan

Editor: Julia van den Hout / Original Copy

Design: Office of Luke Bulman

Managing Editor: Jake Anderson

Image Credits
Aaron Pocock: Cover, 19, 21, 22, 23, 47, 55, 60, 61, 63, 66–68, 70–75, 87, 103, 129, 133, 135, 162, 164–165, 167
Albert Lim: 43, 51, 91-92,
Amir Sultan: 14–15
Darren Yio: 12-13
Patrick Bingham Hall: 59
Peter Mealin: 95–96, 10
Robert Such : 77, 81
All other images courtesy SCDA

First Edition

ISBN: 978-1-951541-31-6

Color Separations and Printing: ORO Group Ltd.

Printed in China.

ORO Editions makes a continuous effort to minimize the overall carbon footprint of its publications. As part of this goal, ORO Editions, in association with Global ReLeaf, arranges to plant trees to replace those used in the manufacturing of the paper produced for its books. Global ReLeaf is an international campaign run by American Forests, one of the world's oldest nonprofit conservation organizations. Global ReLeaf is American Forests' education and action program that helps individuals, organizations, agencies, and corporations improve the local and global environment by planting and caring for trees.